Martin Fido is best known for his popular biographies of Oscar Wilde, Shakespeare and Rudyard Kipling. For twenty years he taught English literature in universities as far apart as Oxford, Michigan and the West Indies. His special field was the mid-Victorian social novel. He has always been interested in true crime, and is currently engaged on a more detailed study of Daniel Good, the Roehampton murderer of 1842.

MARTIN FIDO

Murder Guide to London

GRAFTON BOOKS
A Division of the Collins Publishing Group

LONDON GLASGOW
TORONTO SYDNEY AUCKLAND

Grafton Books
A Division of the Collins Publishing Group
8 Grafton Street, London W1X 3LA

Published by Grafton Books 1987

First published in Great Britain by
Weidenfeld and Nicolson Ltd 1986

Copyright © Martin Fido 1986
Maps by Heather Sherratt

ISBN 0-586-07179-2

Printed and bound in Great Britain by
Collins, Glasgow

Set in Baskerville

For Jacqui
with love and gratitude
always

Contents

Introduction

Crime is a social activity, and inevitably thrives in and around centres of civilization. More than half the memorable murders of Britain have happened in London, and many notable killers have had London associations. Patterns of crime associate with patterns of housing. Murders show which parts of London had the largest servant population. Fraud and bigamy lead to homicide in middle-class areas and western suburbs; street-fighting and gang activities prove lethal in the East End and Clerkenwell. Murder preserves respectability in Holloway: youth kills for kicks in south London.

With this guide and a *London A-Z* it should be possible to find and visit murder sites and places in London associated with major murders. The maps (see Appendix, page 229) show patterns of distribution pictorially and key the reader to murderers' names. The index of names then leads back to an account of the crime and a more precise description of the location in the text. Bold type is used to identify existing murder sites; italic to identify murder sites with obsolete names or house numbers that no longer exist.

The index of places may be used to check immediately what is entered for a street or place known to the reader. Chapter divisions enable an easy survey of the sinister sites in a given locality. Or the whole book may be read as a continuous narrative with detailed accounts of classic cases and the introduction of some forgotten infamous names like Eliza Ross and Edward Dwyer.

The postal districts of London have been allowed to provide the boundaries for this book. (Richmond-based Kate Webster's visits to Hammersmith let her in: Patrick Mahon, living nearby in Pagoda Road, Kew, is out.) But districts have been identified by the parish and borough names that have some colour and point to some local history.

A good deal of the historical integrity of the city's architecture has been preserved. The refurbishing and gentrification of weavers' houses in Spitalfields and Whitechapel still leaves much of the narrow, winding character of the Ripper's streets visible. Cadogan Place still comprises the large houses whose servant population threw up the first convicted murderer of Victoria's reign. Coleby Path and Brunswick Park, Camberwell, tell us something about the aspirations and despair of our own times which can lead to the brutal savagery of bored young sots. Where the actual murder site has been demolished, but the immediate neighbourhood shows a good example of the type of building, this has been noted.

Prior to the nineteenth century, murder normally only attracted attention in its own right if the perpetrator or victim was unusual: the forger Dodd and the murderer Hackman elicited equal attention because they were educated, middle-class and ordained.

The golden age of British murder trials ran from 1830 to 1966. Romanticism made literary figures like Dickens and Browning interested in actions Pope and Dryden would have dismissed as squalid. Since the defendants' lives hung on their outcome (while other crimes were no longer capital) they excited an interest disproportionate to murder's social significance. Acquitted defendants like Mrs Bartlett and uncharged suspects like Mrs Bravo receive as much attention in histories of murder as those who were hanged. Yet throughout this time, the majority of murders were private domestic killings induced by the tension of marriage or disappointed love. Numerous poor Victorian husbands cut their wives' throats in fits of drunken jealousy

(Nathaniel Mobbs at *Enoch Court* off **Goodman's Yard, Whitechapel**; Robert Davis at *11 Dorset Street, St Mary's* – **Dove Road, Islington**, today; Thomas Bare at *33 North Street* – today's **Aybrook Street, Marylebone**; Thomas Corrigan at *Church Street*, **The Minories**; William Lees in **Chapman Street, Stepney**). Poor wives poisoned hated husbands and pocketed their burial money (Anne Merritt at *Peartree Place*, where the Salvation Army hostel stands in Lower Clapton: Mary Wittenbach in *Brill Place*, Somers Town, now covered by Pancras Road). Men and women wiped out their families and themselves in fits of despair (Frederick Finney beside the **Albany Arms, Camberwell**; one Jessup, 'a good and kind man' in Bermondsey; Victor Loynon in **Great Pulteney Street**; surgeon Charles Lewes). Most of them are passed over by history and this book. Their crimes are private and similar.

The Victorian murderer won classic status by unusual violence or the mutilation of his victim; by disappearing and setting off a widely publicized manhunt; by the prominence of his victim or his own respectable status. A cartoon of the 1840s depicted the classic rogues' gallery of that date, and the following table shows how each achieved outstanding notoriety:

Name	Body mutilated	Murder hunt	Famous victim	Middle-class murderer
Greenacre	*	*		
Good	*	*		
Palmer				*
Dalmas		*		
Oxford			*	

(Edward Oxford failed to kill anyone, but by shooting at Queen Victoria and Prince Albert earned his place in the hall of infamy.)

After the Whitechapel terror of 1888, multiple murder and sexual interest could be added to the categories, as may be seen by the figures now standing in the National Criminal Portrait Gallery, Madame Tussaud's:

Name	Body mutilated	Murder hunt	Middle-class murderer	Many victims	Sex
Burke & Hare				*	
Jack the Ripper	*	*		*	*
Peace		*			
Mrs Pearcey					*
Crippen		*	*		*
Smith				*	*
Heath	*		*		*
Haigh	*		*	*	
Christie		*		*	*
Hoseins	(*)	*			
Krays					
Young				*	
Nielson		*		*	
Nilsen	*		*	*	*

It is immediately apparent that Peter Sutcliffe the Yorkshire Ripper must ultimately take his place in the Chamber of Horrors and that the Kray twins are odd men out, representing the late twentieth century fascination with organized crime. Perhaps, too, a wish to make Jack the Ripper the only true five-star murderer explains the endless

-

attempts to ascribe his grisly deeds to some upper-class or royal personage.

One other factor gives lasting interest to murders: protest over the execution, whether because of doubt as to the murderer's guilt, or because the conviction was especially provoking to abolitionists. Indeed, uncertainty about guilt may arouse posthumous interest when the conviction was unremarked at the time (Timothy John Evans).

Cases that are both unfamiliar and commonplace have been omitted: there has been too much murder in London for a comprehensive listing.

I am indebted to the staffs of the British Library and Hackney Central Library.

Stoke Newington/Heamoor, 1985

1

———— The City ————

The old City of London lay on the north bank of the Thames in a semicircular sweep from the Tower of London to Blackfriars. A glance at a street-map shows the outline of the City Wall, repeated in a series of streets.

The west of the City is less clearcut than the east. At Blackfriars the Fleet River joined the Thames, and its progress through Holborn (the 'hollow' passed by the 'burn') along the line of Farringdon Street impeded neat road-building. The jurisdiction of the Lord Mayor and aldermen of London extended further west to Temple Bar in Fleet Street.

Apart from the Tower – which has been used as palace as well as garrison and prison – the royal palaces lay further west, and the administrative capital of the land centred on Westminster and Whitehall, a mile away. London remained a citizens' and not a courtiers' capital.

Hence the distinction between the East End and the West End. While merchants and craftsmen built houses in the fields and villages lying to the east of the City, the gentry and those with fashionable ambitions gravitated to the west, until suburbs west of Westminster itself and more than three miles from old London town had become the aristocratic dormitories.

The City prospered as a market centre. Trade requires a climate of honesty and non-violence (the basis of the despised 'bourgeois morality') and so the activities of

duellists and delinquents tended to take place further west.
It follows that the City of London has had a surprisingly
low murder rate.

Its first notorious murder, a double one, had royal and
political connections: the little princes in the **Tower** were
suffocated on the orders of their uncle, Richard III, in the
fifteenth century. Their bones were found under a staircase
in the seventeenth.

Another murder with royal links – the Overbury affair –
only took place in the City because the Tower was there.
King James I, who had sentimental homoerotic tendencies,
fell for good-looking young aristocrats whose stupidity
never troubled 'the wisest fool in Christendom'. He was
generous to his friends, hence vapid young Robert Carr, a
royal favourite, became one of the most powerful men at
court: a position for which he was totally unfitted.

Carr's private secretary, Sir Thomas Overbury, a slightly
older, wiser man, generally prevented his patron from
committing any gross follies. But his attempt to warn Carr
against a liaision with Frances Howard led ultimately to his
death. Carr fell in love with the beautiful but unscrupulous
Frances Howard, Countess of Essex, and was determined
to marry her if she could obtain an annulment of her
marriage. At the same time, and probably not unconnected,
he slipped a place in the royal esteem.

Overbury opposed the idea of marriage from the start.
Frances, recognizing an enemy, persuaded Carr to arrange
for James to post Overbury as ambassador to Germany –
overtly a mark of royal favour. Overbury correctly saw this
as an attempt to get him out of the way, and refused the
appointment. King James, who resented being crossed,
then committed Overbury to the **Bloody Tower**.

But Frances was not satisfied. She consulted Mistress

Ann Turner of Tyburn (today's Marble Arch), a wise woman who knew something about poisons. She then persuaded Sir Gervaise Elwes, Keeper of the Tower, to turn a blind eye to the transmission of special cakes and pies to Overbury. After receiving these gifts, the luckless secretary died.

The rumour that Overbury had been poisoned spread fast. As a falling favourite Carr had few friends, and the conspirators were soon arrested and brought to trial.

Elwes, Mistress Turner, and the servant who carried in the poisoned food were all condemned to death and executed. Carr and Frances were condemned to succeed Overbury as prisoners in the Tower. After a few years they were released and allowed to live out their lives in provincial retirement.

The next infamous murder in the City was committed by a man who had fallen from a much humbler public office. In 1715 John Price, the common hangman, was committed to the Marshalsea for debt and his position passed to another.

Price enjoyed the privilege known as the liberty of the Marshalsea. He was allowed to leave the prison during the day, provided he returned at night. Early in 1718 he broke this parole and absconded.

Sunday April 13th was a fine spring day, and a great many citizens made holiday in the countryside around Dalston and Kingsland. Hucksters set up stalls in the fields just outside Moorgate, near the **Bunhill Fields** burying ground. At the end of the day Price, returning from his day's outing very drunk, found old Elizabeth White minding her stall and tried to conclude his holiday by raping her. When she resisted he broke her arm and knocked out her eye with his cudgel before passers-by stopped him. Four days later she died. Price was hanged in Bunhill Fields.

In 1732, widowed Mrs Lydia Duncomb was found strangled in her apartment in **Tanfield Court, the Temple**. (An archway opposite the **Temple Church, south of Fleet Street**, is all that remains of the old court today.) Nearby her maid was discovered with her throat cut.

Sarah Malcolm, a young charwoman, was swiftly taken up when she tried to dispose of a silver tankard belonging to the late Mrs Duncomb. She claimed to have been given it as a bribe by the real murderers, but her story was not supported by the discovery of a purse of Mrs Duncomb's coins hidden in her hair!

Sarah's was the most brutal crime hitherto perpetrated by a female. But she was good-looking, as we can tell from Hogarth's portrait of her, and did not lack admirers. The Rev Mr Peddington, who was rumoured to have fallen in love with her, accompanied her in the cart to Temple Gate, where she was hanged.

North of Fleet Street, a delta of little courts debouch from Holborn. *Fleur De Lis Court*, two blocks up Fetter Lane, has recently been swept away in office development. Here Elizabeth Brownrigg became one of the century's most hated murderesses. The Brownrigg family employed workhouse orphans as cheap domestic help and were notorious for ill-treating the unprotected waifs. In 1766 the neighbours spied an imprisoned skivvy through a garret window. They broke into the house and rescued her from the room where she had been kept without food. They were too late. Mary Clifford died after her release, and Mrs Brownrigg was committed for trial with her husband and son. The two men escaped with six months' imprisonment. Mrs Brownrigg was hanged, to howls of execration from the mob.

At **44 East Cheap (on the north side, next to Philpot Lane)** James Burdon kept the *King's Head* public house. His wife's brother-in-law Robert Blakesley was an eccentric young man with a propensity for starting business projects without experience or capital. When he came to Mr Burdon for help, it seemed that he was trying to lay hands on Mrs Blakesley's money. A family quarrel ensued, after which Burdon offered his sister-in-law a home but told Blakesley not to return until he could support himself. Blakesley brooded.

Several times on September 22nd 1841 he told anyone who would listen (including two policemen) that he would kill Burdon if only he had a butcher's knife. Then he went to Aldgate High Street and bought one. He had both edges sharpened at the point, claiming he wanted it for tree-grafting.

At ten in the evening he burst into the almost empty *King's Head*. He stabbed his wife, who was chatting to her sister. He stabbed Mr Burdon, who was snoozing with a silk handkerchief over his head. He hurled the knife over the bar, and ran away.

Mr Burdon staggered to the door and fell prone, part of his intestines protruding from a great gash in his abdomen. Before effective aid could be brought he was dead. Mrs Blakesley was critically wounded. Blakesley disappeared for five days, finally giving himself up to a policeman in Hitchin, Hertfordshire. He was miserable and remorseful.

Soon after her husband's execution, Mrs Blakesley died of her wound. Mrs Burdon ran the pub for a few more years, attracting a massive clientele of sensation-seekers.

In the freezing January of 1845, a small, cross-eyed elderly gentleman in Quaker dress, reading the papers at the Jerusalem Coffee House, Cowper's Court (between 32 and 33 Cornhill) was accosted by a policeman and asked what he knew about the death of a young woman in Slough the previous day. The Quaker claimed that he knew no one in Slough and had not left London. John Tawell attempted to use the novel speed of railway trains to give himself an alibi. By making a parade of leaving his greatcoat at the Jerusalem (really a businessmen's club) he ensured that his presence there at 4.00 P.M. was noted. He then hurried to Paddington Station, took a train to Slough, poisoned the stout he bought for his inconvenient mistress Sarah 'Hunt', caught the next train back to London, and picked up his greatcoat again at 9.00 P.M. The success of the alibi depended on his precise knowledge of train times and the speed with which potassium cyanide killed its victims.

Tawell was foiled by the electric telegraph. A Quaker was seen leaving Sarah's house just before her body was found and the local vicar, with great presence of mind, asked the railway stationmaster to telegraph Paddington, where police spotted the passenger in Quaker dress, trailed him to the Jerusalem and on to the Friends' boarding house at 7 Scott's Yard (between 8 and 10 Bush Lane, running east of Cannon Street station). Next day they made their arrest. It was amazingly swift apprehension of a man who had escaped the scene of crime in a town where he was unknown and had reinstated himself among London's crowds.

Tawell's motive was fear of being found out. Sarah Hadler, a heroine of misplaced love, had declared herself 'dead to the world' five years earlier. She had changed her name to Hunt and abandoned her old associates, including even her mother, because her lover's twin ambitions to marry a genteel Quakeress and enter full membership of the Society of Friends seemed jeopardized by their illicit liaison and Sarah's pregnancy. She moved to Marylebone; to Paddington; to Slough. Tawell paid her a small allowance and at last he poisoned her for fear his wife should learn of her existence.

Mitre Square lies to the east of the City behind Dukes Place, the continuation of Bevis Marks. It is now a little below the street level of the busy traffic junction humming around it where St Botolph Street and Houndsditch converge on Aldgate, giving the impression of a small but open yard. In 1888, with warehouses on three sides and two cottages on the fourth, it was an enclosed court, suitable for open-air prostitution and hence the City's one Jack the Ripper site.

On the night of September 30th Catherine Eddowes, drunk and disorderly on the streets, was taken to Bishopsgate police station (opposite Liverpool Street station). By midnight she had sobered up and was released. She made her way down Bishopsgate and Houndsditch to Dukes Place, and was seen at the covered entrance to Mitre Square talking to a strange man. Half an hour later, the policeman on beat duty found her body huddled in the corner beside Kearley and Tonge's warehouse. Her throat was cut. Her face had been nicked. Her entrails had been pulled out through a long gash running from her breastbone to her abdomen, and part of one kidney had been removed.

This killing became notorious as the Ripper's second within forty minutes. Elizabeth 'Long Liz' Stride had been found in Berner Street, outside the jurisdiction of the City police, less than an hour before. After initial reservations the police chiefs agreed that both killings were the work of the same hand. They were astonished by the speed with which the murderer had made his way from Commercial Road to Dukes Place, and even more surprised by the speed and efficiency of his crime when the officer on beat claimed that he had inspected the empty square a mere fifteen minutes before the body was found.

Two crimes of jealousy and passion in the early twentieth century took place on the open street, signalling the new status of the City as a place where people worked, but did not live. Emma 'Kitty' Byron was the mistress of stock-broker Reggie Baker, and lived with him in lodgings in Duke Street, north of Oxford Street. He was a brutal drunkard who took money from her and beat her. In 1902, on the day of the Lord Mayor's Show, her landlady lost patience with the disorderly lodgers, and evicted Kitty after Reggie had gone to work. Homeless, penniless and despairing, Kitty bought a knife and wandered through the crowds to the city. She found Reggie at the Lombard Street end of **Post Office Court** (an airy covered through-way curving from the Lombard Street post office into King William Street) and stabbed him.

Her misery evoked considerable sympathy at her trial and her reprieve was popular.

Edward Hopwood, a married man who had been carrying on an affair with actress Florence Dudley, shot her in a taxi outside **Fenchurch Street station** in 1912. She had told him earlier that day that their relationship must end. Hopwood failed to kill himself after the murder.

Two other famous twentieth-century murders in the City were the work of gangs.

In 1910, George Gardstein's gang of anarchist immigrants decided to rob H. S. Harris's jewellery shop at 119 Houndsditch (so called because in medieval times the 'ditch' was once choked with dead dogs). The gang rented numbers **9 and 11 Exchange Buildings**, off Cutler Street – the Exchange Club preserves the name – with the intention of breaking through the back of Harris's shop. But they made so much noise that neighbours were disturbed and called the police. With the building surrounded, the gang of seven men and two women rushed out, guns blazing. In an extraordinary incident of sheer havoc they killed three policemen and wounded two others. Gardstein was also wounded – by one of his own side, in error.

Such unheard-of violence ensured their temporary escape. Carrying their injured leader for nearly a mile, they deposited him at lodgings in Grove Street, Stepney, and dispersed. Gardstein died of his wounds two days later, and the police arrested most of his accomplices over the next few weeks. The most sought-after anarchist was Peter Piatkov – 'Peter the Painter'. It was in the hope that they had traced him at last that police and military engaged in the long gun-battle at 100 Sidney Street, overseen by Home Secretary Winston Churchill, which culminated in the discovery of two bodies in the burned-out building. 'Peter the Painter', however, was never found.

The other public murder in the City was again the outcome of attempted theft from a jeweller's. In 1944 Thomas Jenkins and Ronald Hedley, two young hoodlums from the Elephant and Castle, came up to the City to carry out a smash and grab raid in Birchin Lane. As their getaway car made the tight turn from **Birchin Lane** into narrow **Lombard Street**, 56-year-old retired naval commander Ralph Binney stepped out to try to force it to a halt. The desperadoes drove straight at him and, catching him under their car, dragged him for nearly a mile down Clement's Lane and King William Street, across London Bridge, finally dropping his body against the pavement as they turned east into Tooley Street. Hedley was hanged. Jenkins received a long prison sentence.

2

——————— The East End ———————

Immediately to the east of the city lay suburbs running from the Tower to Bishopsgate. Today's long street, The Minories, became part of the borough of Whitechapel (so named when the church of St Mary Mattfellon was painted white).

Originally Whitechapel and its citywards environs, Aldgate and The Minories, were dormitories for workers and craftsmen occupied in London trades. The notion of the 'East End' as a slum area did not arise until the late nineteenth century. London was felt to contain nothing so dreadful as the St Giles rookery until events of the 1880s suddenly focused attention on this new area of overcrowding, poverty, disease and crime.

In the early nineteenth century most Whitechapel householders were quietly respectable, like Mr Burton the optician of *47 Church Street* (today's **St Clare Street**: a cobbled lane running east off The Minories north of Haydon Street, and petering out near the Aldgate bus station). Mr and Mrs Burton planned a neighbourly Christmas. They invited Thomas and Louisa Corrigan to spend the holiday with them, pleasantly close to the Tower and the river. Mr Corrigan was an India House clerk, and a most popular man with all who knew him.

Early in the afternoon of Boxing Day the Corrigans went out to take the air. On their return at 4.00 p.m., Mrs

Corrigan went upstairs to change her dress and Corrigan went with her. Hearing peculiar noises, the Burtons hurried upstairs to find that Corrigan had produced a knife and was busily stabbing his wife to death. Nor was he pleased to be interrupted: he attacked and wounded Mrs Burton.

The event caused no little distress to Mr Corrigan's friends. It was whispered that he had felt some cause for jealousy and, as an extenuating circumstance, he had been drunk.

Goodman's Yard is now merely the sweep of roadway at the south of The Minories by which traffic passes to Mansell Street and Prescott Street. Once it was lined with slum housing and squalid courts. One occupant of *7 Goodman's Yard* in 1831 was the terrifying termagant Eliza Ross. She dealt in cheap skins at 'Rag Fair', the filthy old clothes market in today's Royal Mint Street (then Rosemary Lane). Eliza was believed to acquire her stock by stealing and skinning neighbours' cats.

Before she became notorious as a murderess, Eliza's chief claim to fame was an exploit in the Sampson and Lion, Shadwell, where she quarrelled with the landlady, seized the pub cat, broke its neck, and peeled its skin off with her bare hands.

Her murder was also committed with her bare hands. 84-year-old matchseller Caroline Walsh disappeared, and Eliza was observed hawking her clothes and property about Rag Fair. Eliza's young son revealed that he had watched while his mother held her hand firmly over the old woman's nose and mouth for half an hour, until at last she died. Since Eliza's common-law husband, Edward Cook, had also been present, he was tried with her. But seeing and hearing Eliza apparently convinced the jury that hers was the truly ruling spirit. They accepted his unlikely tale that he had looked steadfastly out of the window for the entire half-hour and seen nothing. He was acquitted.

'The Whitechapel Murderer' was the original title accorded to the unknown 'Jack the Ripper'. Although his murders fell within the tight compass of one square mile, they strayed outside Whitechapel proper to Spitalfields, a region named for a medieval priory and hospital, and developed into attractive streets of elegant houses by refugee Huguenot silk weavers in the eighteenth century. But silk weaving ceased to flourish and by the 1880s the fine eighteenth-century streets had fallen into disrepair: many spaces between them had been filled by wretched brick shacks that could be let cheaply as one-room lodgings.

To the north, on the other side of Bethnal Green Road, lay another slum area of narrow brick streets and blind alleys. 'The Nichol', around Old Nichol Street, was infested by gangs whose livelihood was robbing, mugging and extortion. Whitechapel and Spitalfields were more unsalubrious than unsafe, but the Nichol gangs terrorised the streetwalkers from time to time.

So when the body of Emma Smith was found viciously stabbed outside the cocoa factory at the **union of Brick Lane with Osborn Street** on Easter Monday 1888 the police assumed (probably correctly) that 'Nichol' hooligans were responsible.

August Bank Holiday saw another murder. Martha Tabram or Turner was found on the first-floor landing of a tenement in *George Yard* (today's **Gunthorpe Street**), a narrow alley leading off Whitechapel High Street under a dim arch. Her throat had been cut, and there were a few random stabs in her abdomen. Police soon discovered that Martha and a friend known as 'Pearly Poll' had picked up a couple of soldiers the night before. Pearly had gone off with her client, leaving Martha and the other soldier near

George Yard at midnight. Pearly failed to identify either man in a garrison parade at the Tower.

The discovery of Mary Anne Nichol's body in the gateway opposite Essex Wharf, *Bucks Row* (today's **Durward Street**) on August 31st started the real scare in Whitechapel. 'Polly' Nichol's throat was cut and her abdomen was horribly mutilated. Senior police officers who studied the documentary evidence concluded (a couple of years later) that this was the first actual 'Ripper' murder, but the police carrying out the investigations at ground level, like the general populace, took it for the third.

A week later Annie Chapman's body was found in the back yard of 29 **Hanbury Street**, disembowelled, her throat cut, and her few pathetic coins arranged at her feet. To get to the yard, Annie and her murderer passed through the narrow passageway from the front door of the house in which seventeen people slept. Yet nobody had heard a sound.

The next three weeks were uneventful, and the panic started to die down. Then on September 30th came the double event. The body of tall Swedish Elizabeth ('Long Liz') Stride was found, throat cut, just inside a small court between *Berner Street* (now **Henriques Street**) and **Back Church Lane**, running south off Commercial Road. Apart from a small nick on one ear, there were no mutilations. But it was believed that the noise of the pony trap bringing the secretary of a Jewish Working Men's Club up to the yard (where he discovered the still-warm body) had frightened the murderer away.

Within half an hour yet another murder had been discovered. In **Mitre Square**, just inside the City, a patrolling policeman found the body of Catherine Eddowes.

Panic now rose to hysteria. Sick and silly pranksters chalked messages purporting to come from the murderer around Whitechapel, and sent letters to the police, to news agencies, and to the chairman of the Whitechapel Vigilantes Committee. In these the name 'Jack the Ripper' was first used, although there is little reason to suppose that any of the letters were genuine.

What *was* found on the night of the double murder was a fragment of Eddowes' bloodstained apron, dropped in the entrance of the 'Wentworth Model Dwellings' in Goulston Street (east of and parallel to Middlesex Street, or 'Petticoat Lane') proving unquestionably that the murderer had doubled back from the City boundary into Whitechapel. (The doorways of these dismal and deserted tenements are now sealed up and they are obviously about to be demolished.) On the wall above the apron, the curious message 'The Juwes are The men That Will not be Blamed for nothing' was chalked. It was erased on the Metropolitan Police Commissioner's controversial orders before it could be photographed. Detectives on the ground, however, had seen enough chalk messages around the vicinity to agree that this one was unimportant, and most unlikely to be the murderer's work.

Uniformed and disguised police now crowded the narrow streets of Whitechapel at night. But again there was an interval of inaction. For over a month no bodies were found. Then on November 9th came the worst murder of all. Mary Jane (or Marie Jeanette) Kelly was found so horribly mutilated as to be totally unrecognizable in a wretched room whose floor was slippery with blood and flesh. The room Kelly rented was in *Miller's Court* off *Dorset Street* (now **Duval Street**, but locally unmarked: the open way between Commercial Street and Crispin Street, north of White's Row and the multi-storey cark park.

On this one occasion two neighbours claimed to have heard a woman's voice crying 'Murder!' in the small hours. But the noise of women being abused was so common in the neighbourhood that they paid no attention.

Now the police were deluged with abuse. The Metropolitan Commissioner, Sir Charles Warren, had injudiciously written an article in which he criticized the public for their unimaginative suggestions toward the solution of the Whitechapel murders. If a head was to roll, his seemed to be offering itself, and Sir Charles stepped down from the position he had held for two years.

Yet his fellow chiefs were coming to the conclusion that the Whitechapel murders *were* solved. Robert Anderson, new head of the CID, believed the probable culprit was in an asylum, and he probably satisfied Warren's successor James Monro that this was the case, since intense inquiries died down rapidly.

But police on the ground thought the Ripper was still at large. Two more murders were felt by some ordinary coppers (and the newspapers) to be the work of the Ripper: that of 'Clay Pipe Alice' McKenzie, whose body was found in *Castle Alley* (roughly where the bottom of today's **Old Castle Street** emerges into Whitechapel High Street) in July 1889 and, eighteen months later, the murder of 'Carrotty Nell' Frances Coles, found with her throat cut in **Swallow Gardens**, a sinister space below the dismal railway arches crossing **between Chamber Street and Royal Mint Street.**

To the north, in the Nichol, John Bishop and Thomas Head (the latter's name usually being given as Williams since he only admitted his true identity after the trial) were successfully convicted of suffocating an Italian boy in 1831 to sell his cadaver to anatomists. Before their execution the pair made full confessions: the 'Italian' was actually from Lincolnshire, and was one of three successive victims. The others were an elderly woman and another boy. Their method was to lull their victims with laudanum disguised in rum, and then drown them in a well behind Bishop's house by lowering them headfirst with a rope tied to their feet. The crimes took place in the former *Nova Scotia Gardens*, **between Baroness Road and Columbia Road.**

In 1960, during the gangland competition for control of the Soho rackets, Selwyn Cooney, manager of the New Cabinet Club in Gerrard Street, Soho, was shot dead in the presence of thirty witnesses at the Pen Club in **Duval Street** (the former Dorset Street, which since Mary Kelly's murder had reverted to its ancient name of Duval Street). In spite of all the potential evidence, witnesses were seriously intimidated, and no conviction was reached for anything more than grievous bodily harm.

Flower and Dean Street (now Lolesworth Close), where several Ripper victims dossed occasionally, has associations with Daniel Good (p. 223), Annie Walters (p. 170) and Harry Dobkin (p. 199). Puma Court, further north off Commercial Street near the church, was once Red Lion Court, where Dick Turpin killed his comrade Tom King. But this was accident rather than murder.

Hoxton, to the east of Shoreditch High Street and the Kingsland Road, was almost as gang-infested as the Nichol, but less homicidal. George Woolf's murder of Charlotte Cheeseman (p. 180) on the Tottenham Marshes sprang from their romance in Hoxton. Eagle Wharf Road (between Shepherdess Walk and New North Road) and Avebury Street (a tiny cul-de-sac parallel with Bridport Place facing Shoreditch Park) where Woolf and Cheeseman respectively lived have both had their Victorian terraces replaced by modern council housing. But the Rosemary Branch where Woolf took his doomed girlfriend on the night he killed her still stands, a pleasant old-fashioned little pub, not, as usually described, in Southgate Street, but just off the south end of it on Shepperton Road and Penally Place, heavily overshadowed by the larger, more recent Southgate Arms.

Stepney and Bethnal Green are comparatively flat, dull, run-down territory, broken by the main arteries running east: Whitechapel Road and Mile End Road; Commercial Road, Cable Street and The Highway.

The proximity of the dockland made this last a seaman's area. In 1811 **The Highway** (then the *Ratcliffe Highway*) was the Mecca of sailors ashore, packed with taverns and slop-shops, petty criminals and prostitutes. And in this year it became the scene of crimes that wrung from De Quincey a classic essay on murder.

Mr Marr kept a hosiery at *29 Ratcliffe Highway*, adjacent to Betts Street on the north. The only early buildings now surviving on the entire Highway are two shops on the opposite side of the road, one of them the very attractive bow-windowed no 30. Mr Marr lived in some such building, with his wife and baby. And on the premises he employed a thirteen-year-old apprentice and a servant girl.

On the night of the murder Mr Marr sent the girl out to buy oysters. On her return she found the entire household dead: their heads were battered in and their throats cut. The motive was evidently robbery. But the savagery of the deed and the complete elimination of a houseful of ordinary people horrified the nation.

A week later, the same hand struck again. *The King's Arms* stood toward the upper end of *New Gravel Lane* (today's **Garnet Street**), running from the Ratcliffe Highway to Wapping. Here again, landlord Williamson, his wife and a maidservant were brutally done to death. But this time one person escaped. A young man lodging at the inn heard the noise and saw intruders, and escaped naked from his bedroom window by a sheet. He gave the alarm, but the neighbourhood was unable to prevent the murderers' escape.

Not far away at the Pear Tree Inn in Cinnamon Street, Wapping – the cobbled line of the street remains, but none of its buildings are early nineteenth century – a sailor called John Williams attracted suspicion. A search of his belongings uncovered a bloodstained knife, and the murderer had, to every one's satisfaction, been caught.

Recent research has suggested that Williams may have been framed. But he committed suicide, and was buried with a stake through his heart where Cannon Street Road crosses Cable Street. The murders for which he was held responsible are the ones known as *the* Ratcliffe Highway Murders.

A petty commercial crime took place down the road at no *137* twenty-six years later. John Ready kept a small tailor's shop there, and had friendly business relations with John Pegsworth, the tobacconist at no 69. In December 1837 Pegsworth decided to retire. Ready feared that he might leave the district without paying off a tiny debt of £1 owing to him for a jacket, and he pressed Pegsworth for the money. When the pressure grew intolerable, Pegsworth stabbed him.

Further west, Morris and Marks Reubens committed more traditional assaults on two seamen in 1909. Prostitutes Ellen Stevens and Emily Allen picked up second mate McEarchen and second engineer William Sproull celebrating their shore leave from the *Dorset*. The girls took them to rooms at *3 Rupert Street* (today's **Goodman Street**, parallel to and east of Leman Street between Aldgate and Cable Street. It can no longer be entered; parallel Gower's Walk is similar – cobbled and leading nowhere, though warehouses have replaced hovels). There the Reubens

brothers rushed in, one of them brandishing a hippopoto-
mus-hide stick, and threatened damage to the men who
were assaulting their 'wives'. The Reubens brothers were
in fact ponces who extorted money from punters by blackmail, or simply robbed them while they were at an
unbreeched disadvantage. (This, known as the 'badger
game' in present-day New York, was called 'buttock and
twang' in eighteenth-century London.)

Unfortunately for the brothers, these two seamen, though
very drunk, fought back furiously. The Reubenses pushed
McEachern out of the house, but Sproull gave them
more trouble. Morris therefore produced a clasp-knife and
stabbed him, after which he too could be pushed out. He
staggered over the road, dropping a trail of bloodstained
threepenny bits, and collapsed almost opposite the house.
There he was found after McEachern, drunk and incoher-
ent, had been picked up in Whitechapel Road. The blood
trail led back to the Reubens brothers. The clasp-knife was
discovered ingeniously forced behind a tin plate screening
the wall from the stove. And the fact that it *was* a clasp-
knife hanged the brothers. They could not claim self-
defence or accidental manslaughter in the heat of the fight,
since the need to pause and open the knife proved malice
aforethought.

Such murder in the pursuit of larceny against sailors ashore
was probably the predominating form of unsolved homicide
in the docklands. It was often such an anonymous affair –
'a foreign sailor,' killing 'another foreign sailor' – that
Wapping, Limehouse and (across the river) Rotherhithe
figure surprisingly little in the annals of murder. In May
1911, for example, *The Times* reported that 'a Chinaman'
was killed in **Pennyfields**, Limehouse (then a narrow
alley) by 'three Russian Finns'. The names of murderers
and victim went unrecorded.

Meanwhile the ordinary residential area centring on Mile
End, Stepney Green and Bethnal Green germinated commonplace quarrels and unremarkable murders. In 1833
Robert Emmett, a sixteen-year-old sweep just out of his
apprenticeship, quarrelled with eighteen-year-old paper
stainer George Ashton, and stabbed him in *Globe Lane*
'below the turnpike in Mile End Road' (which stood near
the Sidney Street junction). **Globe Road** emerges into Mile
End Road today: a hundred and fifty years ago it terminated several hundred yards further north.

Just opposite Mile End underground station Rhondda
Road leads north into the tall, narrow houses of Tredegar
Square. In 1874 Henry Wainwright lived at no 40 in this
quiet settlement of the East End bourgeoisie. He had a
brushmaking business in **Whitechapel Road**: a shop at no
84 on the north side next to the old Pavilion Theatre and a
warehouse opposite at *no 215*, backing into **Vine Court** (on
the site of the sixth building between New Road and the
Whitechapel Road entrance to Vine Court).

Nearby at 14 St Peter Street (Cephas Street today,
running parallel to Mile End Road) he met a milliner
named Harriet Lane. He set up love-nests with her success-
ively at no 70 in another St Peter's Street (running along
the line of today's Warner Place from Hackney Road to
Bethnal Green Road), in Bedford Street in the West End,
and finally in Sidney Square back in Stepney.

By 1874 Wainwright had tired of her, and asked his
brother Thomas to impersonate a suitor and woo her away.
(Thomas used the unusual alias of 'Teddy Frieake', which
was considered unfriendly by the real owner of that name,
an auctioneer known to the Wainwrights.)

Which brother finally killed her is not entirely certain,
but Harriet had her throat cut and three bullets fired into
her head before she was buried in the warehouse.

A year after the murder Wainwright's business collapsed. He arranged to give up the Whitechapel Road premises and take cheaper space over the river at Hen and Chicken Buildings, which stood near the junction of Borough High Street with Southwark Street. The smell of Harriet was starting to spread through Vine Court, so he had to take her with him. He exhumed and dismembered her, packing her tidily into parcels which his ex-employer Alfred Stokes helped him carry out to the road. Despite Stokes' objections to the smell, Wainwright left him looking after the luggage while he set off to find a cab. Stokes peeped inside a parcel and discovered a human hand.

Wainwright found his cab and set off for Southwark with the parcels. Across the street he saw Alice Dash, a Pavilion chorus-girl of his acquaintance, and invited her to join him for the ride. He lit a cigar and nonchalantly disregarded the desperate Stokes who was running after the cab hoping to find a policeman. It was not until cab and running man had passed through Aldgate High Street and into Leadenhall Street that any constable appeared, and then two in succession treated Stokes' tale as ridiculous.

The procession travelled over London Bridge and down Borough High Street. When at last the cab stopped a policeman agreed to ask Wainwright what he was carrying in the parcels. Wainwright ensured his immediate arrest by offering the constable £200 to go away and forget about it.

Alice was initially arrested with him, but it was the two brothers who were tried. The jury decided that Thomas was accessory after the fact, and only Henry was sentenced to death. His last days brought out the cynical man-of-the-world. He spent the night before his execution smoking cigars and regaling the warders with tales of his sex-life. And from the scaffold he growled at the hundred or so friends of the sheriffs who had come to witness the execution, 'You curs! So you have come to see a man die?'.

Half-brothers Conrad Donovan and Charles Wade committed a mean shop-robbery in 1904. They attacked Miss Matilda Emily Farmer who ran a newsagent/tobacconist's at *478* **Commercial Road**, tied and gagged her in the backroom, and took her jewellery. A paper-boy found the shop empty, and Miss Farmer's false teeth and one shoe on the floor. When help arrived, Miss Farmer had choked to death on her gag. Accidental homicide consequent on robbery is murder, so Donovan and Wade were hanged.

Most memorable professional crime in Bethnal Green and Stepney after the 1880s was gang-related. But two criminal individualists stand out, forty years apart: William Seaman and John Stockwell.

In 1896, Seaman killed 77-year-old John Goodman Levy and his 35-year-old housekeeper Mrs Sarah Gale. This double killing was famous locally as the 'Turner Street Murders'. It took place at **31 Turner Street, on the corner with Varden Street** (Turner Street runs north-south between Commercial Road and Whitechapel Road, east of New Road, and Varden Street is two blocks north of Commercial Road). Here Levy was reputed to keep the wealth he had amassed as a fence. The house has been converted into a small clothing factory, but no 33 on the other side of Varden Street still stands, and shows exactly what the murder site was like in this district of uniform terraces. The houses are low, two-storey buildings with no basements and have flat parapets concealing their very shallow roofs from the streets. The corner houses present bevels rather than right angles to the pavement corners.

A neighbour saw what looked like a prowler disappearing over the yard wall in Varden Street one evening. Before she had summoned the police, other neighbours observed blood running out under the door. That brought a crowd and the police at once.

The first constables to arrive found Levy's stabbed and battered body just inside the door. Upstairs in the bedroom they found Mrs Gale, also dead, and the room ransacked. But they could not see the 'prowler' anywhere.

This case made the reputation of F. P. Wensley, then a young detective sergeant, and later to be the first Assistant Commissioner promoted from the ranks. Yet, as he himself observed, detection was simple. He had only to look up to see a newly made hole in the bedroom ceiling: he had only to climb on a chair and look through it to see a man disappearing through an equally newly made hole in the roof. Outside on the tiles, the ruffian Seaman realized that he was cornered, and decided to jump, using the gathered crowd to break his fall. Cursing them as Jews, he launched himself earthward, injuring some bystanders and breaking both his thighs in the 40-foot drop.

His final drop was taken in the company of Millsom and Fowler (p. 164). Since these two had been quarrelling ever since their trial, Seaman was hanged between them, observing, no doubt accurately, that it was the first time in his life he'd ever been a bloody peacemaker.

John Stockwell's crime was subtler. In 1934 he murdered the manager of the *Eastern Palace Cinema* in **Bow Road, Mile End**, where he worked, and stole £100 from the safe. He deposited the money at Aldgate East station, and then proceeded to the Suffolk coast where he faked suicide by drowning. But he carried out the details of the 'suicide' unchronologically, so that his clothes were discovered earlier than the postmark on a postcard in which he announced his intention of making away with himself. Naturally this

led to some doubt as to whether he had really died, and he
was soon arrested at the Metropole Hotel, Great Yarmouth.

The Blind Beggar in **Whitechapel Road**, between Whitechapel underground station and Cambridge Heath Road,
is famous as the site of Ronald Kray's murder of George
Cornell. It is worth recalling, however, that the pub was a
gang headquarters seventy years earlier. The 'Blind Beggar
Gang' were the aristocrats of the local mobs. They
eschewed thieving in the poverty-stricken East End, con-
temptuously calling it 'Tom Tiddler's Ground'. Instead
they mugged and picked pockets in the West End and at
racetracks.

They were also capable of violence both in boast and in
deed. They boasted of having once entered their chosen
pub to find it empty save for a commercial traveller. They
told him to leave, threatening to blind him if he stayed. As
he did not take them seriously, one of their number, named
Wallis, thrust an umbrella ferrule through his eye and into
his brain. The victim died in hospital, but an excellent
defence counsel and the supportive testimony of the boys
led to Wallis's acquittal. He returned in triumph to the
East End, drawn in a phaeton by a pair of bay horses. Or
so they said.

The truth was more mundane. The gang had encountered elderly Mr and Mrs Fred Klein on the underground
at King's Cross, and had immediately started making anti-
semitic remarks. The Kleins got out at the next stop (in
1891, **Gower Street**) but the gang followed and tried to
make Fred Klein fight. Ellis (not Wallis), the alias of a 19-
year-old pickpocket whose real name was Paul Vaughan,
stabbed at him with an umbrella. But when he saw that
his victim was seriously injured he ran away, and was
considerably frightened when an arrest for grievous bodily
harm changed to a conviction for manslaughter.

Two equally unfortunate gangsters were Samuel Oreman and Max Moses (better known by his professional boxing name, 'Kid McCoy'), who, at the end of the century, led a mob called the 'Bessarabians' which terrorised all the East End. All, that is, except for one fearless Jewish café-owner named Kikas, who drove the hoodlums off his premises. In his honour, a rival gang named themselves after his 'Odessa' Café, and tried to take over the Bessarabians' territory. Their confrontations grew progressively more violent until, in 1902, the gangs clashed openly at the *York Minster* in **Philpot Street** (running north off Commercial Road, parallel to Turner Street) and an Odessian named Henry Brodovitz was knifed on the street. The leaders McCoy, Oreman and Barnett Brozevishsky received penal servitude for manslaughter.

The 1900s saw the residence of George Gardstein's gang (p. 22) in Stepney. After their disastrous failure to rob Harris's jewellery shop in Houndsditch, the gang carried the injured Gardstein nearly a mile away from the city, down Commercial Road, to the digs he had shared with Peter Piatkov – 'the Painter' – at 59 Grove Street (along the barely detectable line of today's Ropewalk Gardens and Golding Street). Then they dispersed to their own digs in various surrounding streets, the two in no 100 Sidney Street (formerly between Lindley Street and Stepney Way), who may have included Fritz Svaars, dying when the house burned down following the much-publicized shoot-out with the police and military.

It was, by the way, in **Golding Street** – then still *Grove Street* – that Mark Godmacher cut his daughter's throat in 1920 when she and her husband refused to make up a quarrel with him on Atonement day.

But the district's best remembered gangsters are the Kray twins. They were born in Vallance Road (which runs north-south from Whitechapel Road to Bethnal Green Road). They retained their parents' home as a useful headquarters until well into adult life. Like many local predecessors, they were young tearaways who adapted their violence, street smartness and gang loyalty to the protection racket. Like others before them, they offered to hire out muscle as 'enforcers', and thus gained a vicarious entry to West End clubland circles. They were conspicuous in the early 1960s, offering to assassinate unwanted elements in the struggle for control of Soho. They themselves were club-owners – of the 'Two R's' club locally in Bow, and 'Esmerelda's Barn' in Knightsbridge.

Their persistent hankering for recognition differentiated the Krays from the earlier mobsters who had made an adequate living and enjoyed the excitement of racketeering from an East End base. Their love of celebrity and celebrities drew them into the public eye – an unwise place for successful criminals. Their wish to associate themselves with any American Mafia ventures attracted to England by licensed gambling was a rational expansion of business. Their wish to muscle in on the action in Soho was not so. The Krays, after all, would hardly have tolerated an incursion of West or South London mobs into Bow and Bethnal Green. So Ronnie Kray should have anticipated a hostile response when he demanded a slice of the pornography action from George Cornell, sole senior survivor of the Richardsons' South London gang in 1968 after the leaders had been imprisoned. It was tactless of Cornell to call him a 'fat poofter' in reply. Justification on both counts could not disguise the fact that insult was intended. Later Ronnie Kray, who had not made his way up his chosen career without considerable damage to his mental stability, was drinking in The Lion in Tapp Street (off Brady Street)

when word came to him that Cornell was in **The Blind
Beggar, Whitechapel Road**. Kray and a friend hurried
down there, and Cornell had only time to say 'Well, look
who's here' before he was shot between the eyes. ('Ronnie
does some funny things', Reggie remarked when he was
told.)

The pub emptied fast, and as had been normal on such
occasions in the district for decades, neither the barmaid
nor any of the other drinkers had seen exactly what
happened, or felt able to identify Ronald Kray and his
companion.

Reggie Kray was now pressed by his twin to take *his*
man, keeping the pair on an even footing as personal
enforcers. An insignificant member of the gang, Jack 'the
Hat' McVitie, had agreed to undertake a contract murder
farmed out to the brothers and failed. But he was not in a
position to return the advance he had been paid. Hearing
that the Krays had been looking for him in the Regency
Jazz Club, Hackney, he foolishly brandished a shotgun
and made sarcastic remarks about them. It was still more
unwise of him to accept their invitation to a party in a
basement flat in **no 1 Evering Road, Stoke Newington**.
As McVitie bounded down the stairs asking where the
booze and the broads were, he was roughly grabbed. He
tried to bolt through the window, but was pulled back.
Ronnie Kray held him while Reggie stabbed him, his gun
having jammed. The flat was cleaned up, and the body
disposed of professionally. It is reputed to be embedded in
a flyover.

In 1965 Thomas Albert 'Ginger' Marks, described as an
east London secondhand car dealer, disappeared. It seemed
likely that Mr Marks's activities had not been confined to
car dealing. But police enquiries were ineffectual, and the
fate of Ginger Marks was mysterious for ten years.

In 1975 four men were put on trial for his murder. The chief prosecution witness, a Mr Jimmy Evans, had been fortunate enough to win acquittal on charges of shooting and injuring a South Londoner named Foreman in October 1964, and attempting to rob a Bethnal Green Road jeweller's shop in January 1965. Now, in effect, Mr Evans confessed to both these crimes. He claimed that Marks and another man had been involved with him in the dispute leading to Foreman's shooting. He claimed that he and Marks had been rejoining three fellow-thieves at the jeweller's shop between two and three in the morning when they were alarmed by a car which cruised slowly after them. The car followed them along **Cheshire Street** (two blocks south of Bethnal Green Road, between Brick Lane and Vallance Road) and a voice called, 'Ginger! Come here!' As Marks turned, three shots flashed and he fell. Evans dived into the gutter by a nearby public house (The Carpenters Arms and The King & Queen are separated only by a school playground where Cheshire Street parallels St Matthew's churchyard) and saw Marks's legs trailing from the back seat as the car sped off. On the pavement Evans found Marks's hat and spectacles, which he returned to Mrs Marks.

For ten years Evans maintained that he had been unable to recognize the men in the car. Then, meeting one of the murderers in prison, he took fright and identified him to the police.

The judge stopped the trial because he did not feel that Evans's unsupported testimony formed a safe basis for conviction. But he did not disguise his views that the charges had been rightly pressed, and that the possibility of a 'Not Proven' verdict would have been grounds for letting the jury decide.

The underworld belief is that Ginger Marks lies buried in Hackney Marshes. And Cheshire Street, a very dusty row of seedy shopfronts seems a sadly appropriate setting for this story of squalor among thieves.

One famous East End murder was never convincingly attached to the gangs, though the East End underworld persistently hinted that it was the work of anarchists. Steinie Morrison, a professional burglar, spent the latter part of New Year's Eve 1910 in Snelwar's Warsaw Restaurant in Osborn Street with a middle-aged rentier and fence's bagman, Leon Beron. On New Year's morning, Beron's body was found on **Clapham Common**. His head had been savagely beaten in, and long cuts marked his cheeks. His watch and chain were missing, and the £40 or so cash he was reputed to carry was not to be found. Nor was Morrison at his lodgings in 91 Newark Street, south of Whitechapel Road and running into Sidney Street.

A number of people had seen Morrison and Beron walking around Stepney together after midnight, and when Morrison reappeared in the East End a week later, in new lodgings at 72 Fieldgate Mansions, he was arrested at breakfast in Mrs Cohen's restaurant at no 7 Fieldgate Street. None of these actual buildings has survived, but parts of the street still show clearly what they were like.

His absence was easily explained. He had found a new girlfriend, a prostitute nåmed Florrie Dellow, and moved in with her at 116 York Road, Lambeth. But he was arrested on the holding charge of not having reported his change of address to the police, since he was a discharged convict at liberty on 'ticket-of-leave'.

Morrison was identified by three cab drivers. The first claimed to have taken him and Beron from the junction of Mile End Road with Whitechapel Road to the south edge of Clapham Common. The second claimed to have taken Morrison alone from the Battersea side of the common to Kennington cab stand. And the third claimed to have taken Morrison and another, shorter man with a foreign accent from Kennington to Finsbury Park Gate in North London.

Morrison foolishly tried to set up a false alibi. A sixteen-year-old girl from Cleveland Street (now Cleveland Way, running north off Mile End Road beyond the Cambridge Heath junction: a few houses at the top end remain to show how small and crowded they were) had a crush on him. Jane Brodsky had celebrated her sixteenth birthday by having Steinie seduce her in a West End house of assignation, and now swore that she and her sister had seen him at the Shoreditch Empire music hall at the time when he was supposed to have been with Beron in Snelwar's. Unfortunately she was quite unaware that the ticket prices had been raised for New Year's Eve, and that the house was already full at the time when she claimed to have gone there.

Various attempts to prove that Beron's murder must have been committed by anarchists because the cuts on his face looked (to some willing eyes) like the letter S (for spy) were not very convincing, though the underworld subsequently suggested that Morrison had indeed identified Beron to vengeful anarchists in the East End and was not present at the actual murder himself.

The decoy theory of Morrison's involvement would work equally well, of course, if Morrison had helped gangsters to lure Beron down to be robbed in Clapham, where his face could be 'carved' out of earshot of the densely packed East End housing.

In any event, the case against Morrison was sufficiently odd for the Home Secretary to exercise the prerogative of mercy, and Steinie was merely imprisoned. He did not last long, however. Believing himself innocent, he sulked, went on hunger strike, and died while being force-fed. The underworld claimed that exasperated warders had strangled him!

Bethnal Green and Stepney hold two of the Jack the Ripper sites. North of Whitechapel Road, between Whitechapel underground station and Cambridge Heath Road, Brady Street runs up to Dunbridge Street. The second turning to the left off Brady Street is **Durward Street**. This is the old Bucks Row, and Essex Wharf still stands, though the gateway opposite in which Polly Nicholls was found has changed. Berner Street, running south off Commercial Road between Batty Street and Back Church Lane, is now called **Henriques Street**. Half-way down on the right stands a school. Its yard covers the area where the Jewish Working Men's club to the north and cigarette-makers' cottages to the south once lined *Dutfield's Yard*, the little gated court where the Ripper's victim 'Long Liz' Stride died.

There is a connection between Long Liz's murder and another local crime, for a Jewish witness who saw her in the road with a strange man that night was frightened off by the abusive call of 'Lipski', referring to a notorious murder in adjacent Batty Street the previous year.

On 28th June 1887 Miriam Angel was found dead in her locked bedroom at *16* **Batty Street**. Nitric acid had been poured down her throat. Under the bed, unconscious, was Israel Lipski, the attic lodger. He too had swallowed nitric acid.

Lipski accused two journeymen who had been waiting in his room of having attempted to rape young Mrs Angel and kill him. Isaac Schmuss and Simon Rosenbloom of nearby Philpot Street could not give conclusive evidence of their whereabouts at all times that morning, but common sense suggested that it was more probably Lipski who crept in to assault his fellow-lodger and then tried to kill himself. After his conviction he confessed, insisting that robbery rather than rape had been his intention.

In 1849 Patrick O'Connor, the Mannings' victim (p. 186), lived in Greenwood Place, where Maple Street runs south off Whitechapel Road today.

Canal Road runs south of Mile End Road, just east of Mile End underground station. James Greenacre (p. 202) threw Hannah Brown's head over the parapet into the canal at this point and it floated past what were fields in 1836 to jam in the lock-gate half a mile downstream.

3

— From the City to the West End —

West of the City walls, across the valley through which the
Fleet River passed to the Thames and stretching north to
Finsbury fields at the edge of the Islington countryside,
another region of respectable tradespeople's and artisans'
residences developed. The creation of an Italianate piazza
in Covent Garden during the eighteenth century checked
the Holborn spread: the new square was so exclusive
that access was restricted for the first few decades of its
existence.

Like the City itself, Holborn was to pass from being
essentially residential to being largely a business sector,
with corresponding changes in its patterns of murder.
Before the building of Covent Garden, the inhabitants of
Holborn and Clerkenwell lived with easy access to fields:
Clerkenwell Fields; Grays Inn Fields; the fields leading to
Hockley-in-the-Hole (Ray Street). These are sadly over-
built, but in 1635 they were convenient for outdoor prostitution in the summer, and became the working territory of
a lethal 'buttock and twang' partnership.

On April 1st Elizabeth Evans ('Canbery Bess') picked
up randy young Lieutenant Thomas Claxton, at King's
Gate, Bloomsbury (where Gate Street leads into Kingsway
by Holborn tube station). She led him happily off to *Grays
Inn Fields* for dalliance, and once he was unbreeched and
fully attentive to her, Thomas Sherwood ('Country Tom')
crept up and brained him with a large, knobbly iron

cudgel. Then they stripped him of the rest of his clothes, and left him dying.

Two days later Sherwood was arrested in Houndsditch where he tried to sell Claxton's clothes. His interrogation led to Evans's arrest, and hers to the confession that this was their third similar murder. In January that year they had dispatched a merchant named Rowland Holt in *Clerkenwell Fields*, and a year earlier Michael Low had fallen prey to them at the hill leading to *Hockley-in-the-Hole*. Elizabeth expressed penitence before hanging, but Sherwood only regretted having stolen identifiable garments.

The year of Waterloo, 1815, saw the conviction and execution of an attractive young woman who would have been one of the great multiple-poisoners had anyone actually died of her ministrations. Elizabeth Fenning, aged 18, was cook to Mr Orlebar Turner and his family, at *68* **Chancery Lane**. When the entire household, including Elizabeth, was taken sick after dinner one night, it occurred to Mrs Turner that the dumplings had been unusually floury. Elizabeth found herself accused of mixing arsenic in the dumplings, was convicted and hanged. The sentence was deservedly most unpopular. The poor girl probably died because the family had bought some bad meat.

In this region, in 1830, a policeman was killed, the second to be killed in the execution of his duty. PC John Long saw three men behaving suspiciously in Gray's Inn Road one night. He suspected them of casing houses with intent to burgle, and followed them into Theobald's Road, along Lamb's Conduit Street into Guildford Street, back in the direction of Gray's Inn Road again, and north into **Mecklenburgh Square**. There he approached them directly. Two of them made off: the third, William Sapwell (who called himself John Smith) stabbed him.

Mount Pleasant Sorting Office stands directly on the site of *Coldbath Fields Prison*. George John Hewson was lucky to be alive serving a sentence even in this notoriously severe gaol in 1840. He had been convicted of concealing the death of a baby born of his incestuous relationship with his daughter: they both might easily have been topped for infanticide.

But his good fortune did not reconcile Hewson to the regimen of the long slow shock. William Woodhouse, one of the warders, had him sent to a punishment cell. When Woodhouse came into the yard a little later, Hewson hurried out of his cell concealing his right hand with a pannikin held in his left. When he reached Woodhouse, he dropped the pannikin and stabbed him with the knife he had been hiding. He felt no remorse. His attitude was expressed in his remark as he was led away: 'It has served the bloody villain right. I only wish Warder Latham was in the way, and I would have served him in the same way.'

In 1868 the same prison was the scene of an incident leading to the last public execution in England. A group of Fenians exploded barrels of gunpowder beside the wall of the exercise yard, hoping to free some imprisoned comrades. But the authorities had been warned and the prisoners were not exercising. Nevertheless four innocent passers-by were killed.

Michael Barratt was arrested in Liverpool. He may not have perpetrated the explosion: a much taller man had been observed setting light to the fuse. And Barratt's courage and dedication to his political beliefs made a good impression in court. Nonetheless this impenitent Fenian was hanged.

A tenderer homicide with a milder outcome took place on the other side of Farringdon Road in 1911, when Charles

Ellsome apparently stabbed Rose Pender in **Wilmington Square**. He was twenty-two: she was nineteen, and the course of true love had gone badly awry. Ellsome's defence was a weak alibi. The jury had little difficulty in finding him guilty. But the prosecution had used a dubious 'confession' he allegedly made in prison to an epileptic fellow-convict as its weightiest evidence against him. The Court of Appeal overturned the verdict.

In the tangle of streets where Holborn Viaduct overruns Farringdon Road to eliminate the once-notorious gradient of Holborn Hill, an inn called *The Golden Anchor* used to stand at the junction of **Saffron Hill** with *Castle Street*. Here in 1865 a brawl broke out between Italian immigrants and xenophobic Londoners. A knife was drawn, and in a moment one of the Englishmen, Michael Harrington, lay dying.

An Italian named Serafino Pelizzioni was arrested, despite his countrymen's protests that he had only come in from The Three Tuns over the road to make peace. When an anti-Italian jury went so far as to convict him, the Italian community found the true culprit, one Gregorio Mogni, who willingly gave himself up.

But the police had closed the file and refused to re-open it. Rather than see Pelizzioni punished for his crime, Mogni submitted to a private prosecution, and forced justice out of an unwilling Britain.

Holborn Viaduct, Holborn and High Holborn follow the route of the condemned felon from Newgate to Tyburn Road (Oxford Street). **Almost at the St Giles end of High Holborn**, on the south side, Dorothy Wallis ran a secretarial employment agency in 1946 at no 157 (since rebuilt, but a number of old three-storey office buildings in the area remain). With her little office on the top floor,

36-year-old Miss Wallis was a successful self-employed businesswoman. It was a shock to her secretary to come in for work at 9.00 A.M. one day and find her employer's bloodstained body lying before the desk. An educated man's voice had answered the office telephone at 6.00 P.M. the night before, and gently put the caller off. At around 6.30 P.M. screams had been heard. Examination of Miss Wallis's diaries revealed that she had been a pioneer of late-night cruising 'looking for Mr Goodbar'. The murder was never solved.

Gray's Inn Road gained some notoriety again in 1950, when Socrates Petrides, a waiter who lodged at **no 57**, went cruising in one of the Soho homosexual cafés. He had the misfortune to turn his attention to a young provincial student, Michael Hardisty, who had missed his last train to Blackpool, and did not realize the nature of the café or the purport of Petrides' kindly offer of a bed for the night. When they arrived at the flat in Gray's Inn Road, and Petrides' intentions became apparent, Hardisty furiously fought off his advances. In the struggle, Petrides seized an ornamental samurai sword from the wall to defend himself, and killed Hardisty. He was convicted of manslaughter.

The development of the Covent Garden piazza encouraged the development of service trades in the abutting area. But the presence of the Opera House and the Theatre Royal, Drury Lane, also provided, as puritans would have predicted, a focal point for prostitution. Citizens enjoying a night out might easily be persuaded to make it a night on the tiles. This trade was supported by Covent Garden market, whose carriers and drovers brought in not only country produce, but also country girls looking for employment in London. Procuresses met the new arrivals and offered them lodgings, thus recruiting new faces and, possibly, virginities, for which there was a market.

A rabbit warren of long, low, more or less disreputable streets ran from the notorious thieves' kitchen of St Giles to the more open space of Covent Garden. Stukeley Street, at the north end of Drury Lane, contains a couple of old houses giving some impression of the monotonous small brick dwellings that filled the area. Seven Dials, where Mercer Street, Monmouth Street and Earlham Street cross each other, with Short's Gardens joining the convergence, was a notable curiosity a hundred and fifty years ago, as a small open space from which the seven narrow alleys seemingly ran to nowhere.

Stukeley Street witnessed mob activity in 1748. It was known then as Coal Yard. It had declined somewhat from the decent petit-bourgeois neighbourhood in which Nell Gwynn was reputed to have been born in the seventeenth century, but had not yet become the foul slum that it was by the mid-nineteenth. In the 1740s, it housed John Thrift, the public hangman. After Bonnie Prince Charlie's Highland Rising of 1745 it fell to Mr Thrift to behead the rebel lords instead of merely suspending them. And while the city fathers of London thoroughly approved, the vulgar citizenry were offended by the bloodshed, impressed by the dignity of the victims, and not averse to a little mischievous Jacobitism. An angry crowd chased Thrift to his house and besieged it, shouting Jacobite slogans.

Once home Thrift recovered his nerve and lost his temper. Seizing a cutlass, he rushed out of the door and set about the mob, which fled before him, crossed Drury Lane and raced into **Short's Gardens**. There followed a brief mêlée at the end of which one David Farris was seen to be lying dead, felled by Thrift's cutlass. The hangman was taken up on a charge of murder.

He submitted that the cutlass had been seized from his

grasp by Enoch Stock, who had actually struck down Farris. And Stock did not contest this, averring that he had been stunned in the brawl and had no idea what had happened.

This availed Thrift nothing. He was condemned to death. However, the City fathers had no intention of seeing Jacobitism endorsed by mob action. They petitioned for Thrift's reprieve, and on his next visit to Tyburn he was, as usual, putting the rope around some one else's neck instead of wearing it himself.

By 1821 *Coal Yard's* reputability was sinking. It now housed the parish constable, Mr Haffan, but he let the property next door to a very dubious couple: Matthew Welch and Mary Baker. Both were married: Mr Welch had a wife and children in Paddington, while Mrs Baker's husband lived in the country. Trouble started when Mr Baker paid a visit to his estranged wife. He left before Welch's return, but a drunken Welch quarrelled so furiously with her for having entertained her legitimate spouse that the neighbours intervened and threatened to lock him up in the watch-house. Welch drove them out with a poker, and at midnight barricaded himself in the house with his paramour. Until one o'clock the horrified occupants of Coal Yard listened to curses, blows and screams. Then an ominous silence fell. But nobody dared to investigate until the next morning when Mary Baker Welch was found on her bed with her brains beaten in. Of her common-law husband there was no sign.

Enquiry revealed that he had calmly turned up for breakfast with his legal family in Paddington. It was, under the circumstances, unsurprising that he did not tell them where he was going after he had eaten. And no one heard of Mr Welch again.

At this time (1820s) St Giles parish had the dreadful
reputation it was to hold until mid-century. The infamous
'rookery' lay under today's Centre Point. Dyott Street and
Grapes Street (then Vine Street) were access roads to it.
The sordid nature of St Giles criminality was well exhibited
by one Joseph Connor, who passed an evening early in
1845 walking up and down Vine Street (Grapes Street),
Little George Street (directly under today's Centre Point)
and New Oxford Street, accosting various acquaintances
and passing prostitutes, and asking them whether they
knew a woman called Mary Brothers, whether they thought
she would recognize him, and abusing her for having given
him gonorrhoea. At one point he hurried away home and
changed into a velveteen suit, and then returned to repeat
his questions. One elderly whore who knew him as a
former client examined him at his request for signs of
disease but found none.

Having made his presence and his interest in Miss
Brothers thoroughly familiar to the entire neighbourhood,
Connor went to the cutler's shop at 10 St Giles High
Street, kept by Mr Oldham, and bought a large knife.
With this he hurried back to find Brothers, took her to a
threepenny room in Mrs Hale's brothel at *11 Little George
Street*, and stabbed her in the neck before forcing his way
out and disappearing in the direction of Drury Lane.

A few days later he was traced to the house of his aunt
Mrs Leonard at 4 Stonecutters Alley, off Gate Street (next
to Holborn underground station today). Here a wholly
new explanation of his crime was proposed. Connor, who
was only twenty, had for some time been keeping company
with his young cousin Margaret, and it had not been
conducive to the course of this romance that 46-year-old
Mary Brothers visited the house looking for him.

Connor's case was unusual in that he had made such an
exhibition of himself and his grievance prior to the murder

that he ensured his own hanging. He died an exemplary young penitent, confessing that his motive had been revenge for the venereal disease he wrongly thought Brothers had passed to him.

To the south, Covent Garden did not endure the same utter degradation, though there was a seamy district between Covent Garden and the Strand which included the capital's principal pornography publishers and the home of gambler William Weare, who was the subject of a famous broadsheet ballad stanza after he had been murdered by his friends Thurtell and Hunt. They lured him out for a weekend's shooting in Essex and – in the words of the ballad –

> His throat they cut from ear to ear;
> His head they battered in.
> His name was Mr William Weare
> What lived in Lyons Inn.

Covent Garden's most famous murder occurred as the fashion for 'sentiment' was growing, and the Reverend James Hackman inspired the sort of sentimental tears that Laurence Sterne was suggesting were elegantly moral.

In 1774 Hackman was a young lieutenant of the 68th Foot. In that year he met Margaret Reay, kept mistress of the Earl of Sandwich for whom she had born several children. They fell in love. But Hackman was unable to support her, and she felt a continuing loyalty to Sandwich. The affair seemed hopeless, and early in 1779 Hackman left the army and took holy orders. One night in April he saw Miss Reay passing through Whitehall. He followed her, unnoticed, and discovered that she was going to Covent Garden to see *Love in a Village*. With the desperation of his love rekindled, Hackman hurried home and fetched a pair of pistols intending, he said, to shoot himself before her eyes.

In fact he shot her in the theatre portico in full view of the emerging audience.

The romantic story thrilled everyone. Sandwich, with a sense of sublime forgiveness, no doubt, assisted Hackman financially through his imprisonment and trial. Dr Johnson and Topham Beauclerk argued about the merits of the case. Boswell, whose emotional exhibitionism always outweighed whatever shreds of good taste he possessed, accompanied Hackman to the gallows in the mourning coach which a gentleman cleric could use in preference to the ordinary felon's cart. Altogether, it was a thoroughly affecting, genteel and silly business.

British theatre's most famous murder occurred near this kindergarten of theatreland. William Terriss (born William Lewin) was a popular actor-manager of the 1890s, specializing in light comedy thrillers. He was a genial man-of-the-world, much liked for his generosity. And he was notably kind to an unstable Scottish actor named Richard Prince. Terriss found him work, gave him recommendations, and lent him money with little expectation of seeing it returned.

Prince repaid this kindness with fits of increasing moodiness and stormy scenes. It became impossible for Terriss to employ him; in the end it became difficult for Terriss to receive him.

On December 13th 1897 Prince was refused a complimentary ticket at the Vaudeville Theatre in the Strand, adjacent to the Adelphi which Terriss leased. He made an outrageous scene, and returned to his lodgings near Victoria to brood. Blaming Terriss for his rejection at the theatre, he came to blame his benefactor for all his sufferings, his present unemployment and poverty.

Three days later Terriss arrived for work at the Adelphi

Theatre. **The stage door of the Adelphi** is in **Maiden Lane**, south of Covent Garden and parallel to the Strand. It is a quiet street, housing Rule's famous restaurant, and a Catholic church which serves as the home of the Catholic Theatre Guild. Almost opposite Rule's, two doors in a yellow stucco wall, one of them rather splendidly surrounded, are the stage doors to the Adelphi Theatre. Terriss used the more westerly of these as his private entrance. He dismissed his cab at the end of Maiden Lane and enjoyed the walk to the door. As he turned to its step, Prince, who had been lurking across the road outside Rule's, rushed over and stabbed him. Terriss died outside his own theatre, to the distress of the profession.

Prince's behaviour in court was bizarre, and evidence revealed that he had long been known as 'Mad Archie'. He was found guilty but insane.

Cecil Court, a pedestrian way of secondhand book and print shops, lies between Charing Cross Road and St Martin's Lane. Louis Meiers' antique shop was still there until a year or two ago, charmingly dusty and old-fashioned so that one wished to call it a curio shop.

There in 1961, young Eurasian Edwin Bush stabbed assistant Mrs Elsie May Batten with two antique daggers and a sword. He claimed in court that she had made a racist remark – but he had previously admitted that he killed her to obtain the sword.

He was the first murderer to be traced after the issue of an Identikit picture (the hand-drawn predecessor of Photofit) assembled from witnesses' descriptions.

Twentieth-century Covent Garden and St Giles have been extensions of twentieth-century Soho, as far as murder is concerned. Like neighbouring St Giles and Leicester Square, Soho was earliest recognized as an area of fields.

Its name is reputed to come from the calls of hunters riding across them.

The present-day sleaziness of the square mile and the extent of the strip-clubs and prostitutes' flats make it convenient to see Gerrard Street and Lisle Street of the former Leicester Fields region as part of Soho too.

Some observers trace its reputation as a haunt of prostitutes to its early days, but in fact Portland Town (as the development of the Duke of Portland's land west of Soho Square was known until the name was re-used for the family's subsequent development to the northwest of Regent's Park) was dully respectable compared with its neighbours, St Giles, Seven Dials and Covent Garden.

The unfortunate William Bousfield of *9 Portland Street* (now **Noel Street**), rated a broadsheet in the early years of Victoria's reign when he stabbed his wife and two daughters (aged 6 and 4) and the baby, before giving himself up to the police. His was obviously a domestic murder of despair, Bousfield seeing no way of continuing to support his family. His hanging was appallingly bungled by the incompetent Calcraft: Bousfield's drop was so short that he swung his feet back on to the scaffold four times before Calcraft descended into the pit and dragged him down.

The eastern end of Noel Street has been completely redeveloped, but a few houses in nearby Portland Mews give an impression of the small, brick-built, artisans' cottages which constituted the more downmarket parts of Portland Town.

In 1843 Michael Stöltzer killed bootmaker Peter Keim of Dean Street quite openly in *Broad Street* (now **Broadwick Street**). Both were immigrant Germans, and Keim had just taken some bread and butter to the indigent Stöltzer.

–

The Prussian Kaiser expressed concern over the case, and the evidently mad Stöltzer was reprieved.

In the twentieth century, ease of access from Piccadilly Circus and Leicester Square made the district a desirable source of small working flats for street prostitutes. The need for a system whereby foreign whores wishing to work in the rich market of Central London could obtain passports through arranged marriages, the difficulty of letting flats without being charged for brothel-keeping, and the presence of tight-knit immigrant communities all combined to bring the trade under the dominance of effective organized crime.

The first evidence that homicidal violence was an aspect of this thriving business came in 1936, when a middle-aged pimp known as 'Red Max' or 'Ginger Max' Kassel – his real name was Emile Allard – was shot in prostitute Suzanne Naylor's (or Bertron's) flat at **Little Newport Street**, the row of small shops between Lisle Street and Charing Cross Road. Kassel quarrelled over a small debt with Suzanne's live-in ponce Georges Lacroix and Pierre Alexandre, the landlord of the flat. Lacroix did the shooting, and then he and Alexandre dismembered the body and drove it to St Albans where they dumped it on the golf course, while Suzanne and her maid Marcelle Aubin cleaned up the flat very efficiently. But they found it necessary to trim off the bloodstained curtain hems, and this incongruous feature caught the attention of sharp-eyed police making routine enquiries among Kassel's known associates. Lacroix fled to France, where he was arrested and sent back to Devil's Island, from which he was an escapee. Alexandre was condemned to five years' penal servitude for his part in the affair.

It has long been suggested that intimidation and the threat of murder are used to control prostitutes who do not want to hand over a percentage of their earnings. The shooting of 'Black Rita' Barrett in her flat in **Rupert Street** in 1947, and the knifing of Rachel Fenwick a year later in her flat immediately opposite the police accommodation for unmarried constables, Trenchard House in **Broadwick Street**, were both suspected to be disciplinary measures by vice bosses, but no charges were ever brought. The mysterious death in 1948 of 'Russian Dora' – 60-year-old Helen Freedman – in her flat in **Long Acre, Covent Garden** also appeared to be disciplinary control of an active prostitute.

The famous boxer Freddie Mills invested much of his earnings in a Chinese restaurant at 143 Charing Cross Road during the 1940s, and as this gradually became unprofitable, he changed the premises to a club which he optimistically intended to be a place for family relaxation. With a certain naïvety, he assumed that 'hostesses' need not be on the game, and when his club was attended by the notorious Kray twins he accepted their assurance that they were much-maligned businessmen. In 1965 his body was found in his car in **Goslett Yard**, a tiny court running towards Soho off the northern end of Charing Cross Road. The inquest maintained that he had committed suicide with the shotgun found beside him. His family and friends never believed that this courageous and humane man would have inflicted such shock upon those he loved, and remain convinced that he was murdered as a warning to other club owners who resisted extortion.

To the prostitute, however, the customer is a more familiar hazard than the manager. Lou Harvey, who gave important evidence against Neill Cream (p. 189), was taken by him to a hotel at the Oxford Street end of Berwick

Street in 1892. And Gordon Frederick Cummins (p. 65) revived a nasty nineteenth-century custom by cutting the throat of Evelyn Oatey before mutilating her body in her flat at **153 Wardour Street**.

Frederick Field (later – 1936 – hanged for the murder of Beatrice Sutton at **Elmhurst Mansions**, Clapham) was tried in 1933 for the murder of Norah Upchurch. Her body was found in the basement of **173–9 Shaftesbury Avenue**, a shop backing on New Compton Street close to St Giles High Street. Field was a sign-fitter who had been given the empty shop keys by his employers. When the street-walker's strangled body was found on the premises, Field was questioned as the last person known to have visited them. He told an elaborate tale of having given the keys to a man in plus-fours with a gold tooth who claimed that he had an order to view and offered Field work in rewiring the shop. Field even identified a stranger in custody at the police station as the man: but Field's identificatee had no gold teeth.

This improbable story and the lack of any direct evidence linking Field with Upchurch inhibited prosecution until Field sold a confession to the newspapers. He was promptly charged.

He withdrew his confession at the trial; it had not accurately described Upchurch's death in any case (claiming that she had been strangled by his bare hands, whereas her belt had been used as a ligature). He was acquitted.

After this escape Field joined the RAF, but the life of discipline did not suit him and he deserted. He was arrested for desertion in Clapham Manor Street. And on his arrest he confessed to the murder of Miss Sutton, whose strangled body had been found in her flat. Once again Field tried to withdraw his confession at the trial, but happily the jurors did not let renewed doubts license Field to continue his horrible hobby. He was convicted.

A large modern block now occupies the site of the more old-fashioned shop where Miss Upchurch's body was discovered. But a glance across the road shows what upper Shaftesbury Avenue was like in the days of open street prostitution in central London.

In 1946 a 26-year-old ex-borstal girl named Margaret Cook was shot in an alley by the Blue Lagoon Club in **Carnaby Street**. Though a friend had warned her that a young man she was seeing had a gun, she had ignored the warning, and the man was never identified or traced. All that could be proved was that the murder had nothing to do with the club by whose name it became known.

The 'West End' of town has shifted as the town has grown. For Defoe it was Fleet Street: a hundred years later it could describe almost anywhere in Westminster or Marylebone. But in popular usage for the last hundred years, it has generally referred colloquially to the central shopping and theatre streets of the capital: a looping trail from the Strand through Trafalgar Square and Leicester Square, taking in Lower Regent Street and the Haymarket to Piccadilly Circus, and ending with Regent Street and Oxford Street.

Oxford Street was formerly *Tyburn Road*, leading to the village of Tyburn on the edge of open countryside at Marble Arch. Mistress Anne Turner, the dyer and poisoner employed by Sir Robert Carr and Frances Howard (p. 16) to help with the murder of Sir Thomas Overbury was a resident of Tyburn.

Catherine Hayes and her husband lived in *Tyburn Road* until 1725. They took lodgers – two young men named Wood and Billings – and regrettably Mrs Hayes came to prefer them to her husband. Hayes was successfully deceived, and was persuaded to go drinking with the

–

household at the Brawn's Head Inn, New Bond Street. When he was incapably drunk, they escorted him home, where he was battered to death with an axe and dismembered. They threw a bucketful of his blood down a well, dumped his head on the Thames' mud at Horseferry Passage (where Lambeth Bridge now crosses the river) and other parts of his body in a pond in Marylebone Fields.

The head was picked up at Millbank, taken to St Margaret's churchyard (under the shadow of Westminster Abbey) where it was placed on a tombstone, and later raised on a pole for anyone to identify. Friendly neighbours suggested to Catherine that this might be her husband. Her refusal to make the identification only delayed her exposure and conviction.

She established two records. She was the first murderer to be caught as a result of strewing bits of body around London. And she was the last to be burned at the stake for 'petty treason' – the murder of a husband.

Thereafter **Oxford Street** was remarkably free from murder until the tragic event of 1945, when young Jack Tratsart shot his father and sister in the sorely missed *Lyons' Corner House* on the north side of Oxford Street near the Tottenham Court Road end. A family party was celebrating the lad's birthday, but Tratsart, sadly convinced that they did not really love him, tried to kill the entire group including himself. He made no attempt to evade arrest, but sullenly refused to tell the police what had become of the pistol. All the other diners had hidden under the tables when the shooting started, and no one had observed Tratsart's extraordinary success in throwing the weapon into a hanging lightbowl without breaking it. He was clearly the victim of overwhelming depression, and was mercifully confined to Broadmoor.

The **Café Royal**, haunt of wits and artists from Oscar
Wilde's day to Peter Warlock's, is near the south end of
Regent Street. In its heyday, the Café Royal enjoyed its
very own murder. Marius Martin the nightwatchman was
found lying just inside the **Glasshouse Street** side entry to
the premises on the morning of December 6th 1894. He
had been shot in both sides of the face. There were no signs
of a struggle or a break-in. The circumstantial evidence was
that someone had stayed hidden in the building after it
was closed: reports from staff suggested that one of the
men's lavatories near the passage might have been occupied
while the last waiters were leaving.

Martin had many enemies. He was a sour busybody
who had brought about the dismissal of several fellow-
employees by reporting them if he saw them carrying
anything out of the building. His murderer was never
discovered.

Glasshouse Street almost abuts on **Denman Street**, behind
Piccadilly Circus and Shaftesbury Avenue. Pioneer aviator
Julian Hall had a flat there just before the first world war.
He shared it with a young lady named Jeannie Baxter,
who had previously lived with him in Carlton Mansions,
Maida Vale. Their relationship was stormy, and eventually
Jeannie shot him. She had the good fortune to be defended
by Marshall Hall. The handsome advocate was at his best
working for good-looking ladies in fashionable circles. He
was also skilled at persuading juries that guns were dangerous things, liable to go off accidentally. In this case he
argued convincingly that Miss Baxter had intended to kill
herself, rather than her lover.

Piccadilly Circus was visited by Percy Thompson and his
wife Edith on the last night of his life. They came up from
Ilford to see Hermione Gingold and Binnie Hale in Ben

Travers' *The Dippers* at the Criterion Theatre. Back in
Ilford that night as they walked toward their house Edith's
lover Frederick Bywaters rushed out of the shadows and
stabbed Mr Thompson. Mrs Thompson, too, was executed
for this crime despite a storm of protest. For her passionate
but indiscreet letters to Bywaters had contained silly fantasy claims of her own attempts to poison her husband,
and could have incited the young man whose love was as
intense as hers.

Just south of Piccadilly Circus, Jermyn Street runs between
Lower Regent Street and the Haymarket. Parallel with
these main roads, St Albans Street runs south off Jermyn
Street, joined to the Haymarket by tiny Norris Street. The
Captain's Cabin, on the corner of Norris Street and St
Albans Street, was the scene of the assault which finally
brought Gordon Frederick Cummins to justice.

This mass-murderer and mutilator would be far better
known had his crimes not taken place in wartime, when
paper rationing prevented extensive reporting. Cummins
usually attacked lone women under cover of the black-out.
But he was interested in robbery as well as sexual release
through violence, and his first victim was a respectable
schoolmistress in Marylebone. Early in 1942 Evelyn Hamilton was strangled in an air raid shelter in **Montagu Place**
and her handbag was stolen.

The crime was so different from the throat-slitting and
mutilation of Soho prostitute Evelyn Oatey in her **Wardour
Street** bedroom that the same hand was not apparent.
Oatey's death was, however, obviously similar to that of
Margaret Lowe, who was found strangled and mutilated in
her flat, no 4 in the block **9–10 Gosfield Street** (in the
Great Portland Street region between Regents Park and
Upper Regent Street). Probably Oatey and Lowe both

picked up Cummins on West End beats before taking him back to their flats.

So did his next victim, Doris Jouannet, who was well-known to pick up servicemen in pubs around Leicester Square. Her flat was well to the west, at **187 Sussex Gardens, Paddington**, and here she was found, strangled and mutilated.

As 1942 drew towards a close Cummins overreached himself. He picked up a Mrs Greta Heywood near Piccadilly, and had a drink with her in the Trocadero Hotel. From there they went on to the Captain's Cabin, where Cummins attacked her in the blacked-out street. But Mrs Heywood resisted fiercely, and Cummins ran off into the Haymarket leaving his gas-mask in her hands.

This was the end for him. A survivor could now describe her attacker as an airman, and he was traced and identified through the gas-mask.

Still he made one last attempt to kill before his arrest that night. He picked up Kathleen King whose real name was Mulcahy and who, like Doris Jouannet, took West End clients back to a Paddington flat. They travelled by taxi to 29 Southwick Street, where Cummins made his last assault. She screamed and struggled, and, his nerve shattered by the earlier experience with Mrs Heywood, he ran away.

The cheap nylons he used as ligatures lent linguistic glamour to his crimes: 'The Silk Stocking Murders' gave a false impression of sophisticated high life in a dreary world of clothing coupons.

Leicester Square grew out of *Leicester Fields*. A quite pioneering murder was committed here in 1761 by the Frenchman Theodore Gardelle, whose house stood close to Sir Joshua Reynolds', on the west side of the square, just north of Panton Street. Gardelle was one of the earliest murderers to dismember his victim in order to dispose of the remains more easily around his own premises. He killed his landlady Mrs King: by some accounts in order to rob her, by others because his repeated attempts at seduction annoyed her, and when he went on to attempt rape she found herself to be much the stronger and beat him up. Gardelle retaliated lethally with a poker.

Having a body on hand, Gardelle paid off the maid and shut up the house for five days while he laboriously carved up Mrs King with a clasp-knife. The work done, he hired a charwoman to help him clean up, but her work was hindered by a blocked cistern in which she found a quantity of 'meat' and some blood-soaked blankets. Bow Street Runners, on investigating, found more blood and flesh inside the house.

Surprisingly Gardelle did not pioneer the defence put up by most subsequent dismemberers to the effect that Mrs King had died accidentally, and he disposed of her body 'in a panic'. He was hanged in Panton Street.

A nasty aristocratic crime took place in *Howard Street*, which until recently ran south from The Strand **in between Arundel Street and Essex Street**. Mrs Anne Bracegirdle was the toast of the Restoration stage in 1692. Actresses were believed to be unusually promiscuous, and Mrs Bracegirdle was not one of the rare fair Thespians with a reputation for extraordinary chastity. Lord Mohun's friend Captain Hill wished to sleep with her. He believed, wrongly, that actor Will Mountfort was her permanent lover, and assumed, crassly, that if Mountfort were eliminated Mrs Bracegirdle would submit to him. So Mohun and Hill stopped Mountfort in Howard Street one night. Hill slapped his face, and ordered him to draw his sword before running him through. This could be presented as a duel following on a quarrel; mere manslaughter at worst.

Sudden death in the **Savoy Hotel, the Strand**, two hundred years later also had a gamey flavour of 'high society'. One of Marshall Hall's greatest triumphs was his defence of French-speaking Madame Fahmy Bey, who was literally found with a smoking pistol in her hand beside her husband's dead body in their suite in 1923. The case was tailor-made for a repetition of Marshall Hall's triumph with Jeannie Baxter: he could and did claim that Mme Fahmy had only picked up the pistol to threaten suicide.

What made the case distasteful was his consciously racist effort to evoke sympathy for Mme Fahmy by blackening the character of the dead man. There could be little doubt that the lady had married Prince Fahmy Bey for his money and his title; that she had little or no interest in Islamic culture, and was completely unprepared for the secondary and ornamental role she was to play in his life. The marriage was unhappy for her. She had no security, as she could be divorced and left penniless at Fahmy's whim. She was very jealous of her husband's secretary and close friend, Said Enani, and allowed Marshall Hall to hint (without evidence) that the relationship between the two men was homosexual.

Worse still was the exposure of Mme Fahmy's own bedroom sufferings. She produced medical testimony to her piles and fistula, and claimed that not only were these caused by her husband's habit of sodomising her, but he went on doing so even after the ailments made the practice agonizing.

Worst of all was the calculated attempt to suggest that sexual deviation and brutality were only to be expected from 'non-white' foreigners and that all 'orientals' secretly wanted to bugger and bully defenceless European maidens. Marshall Hall's client was acquitted triumphantly. And the Egyptian Embassy made a perfectly valid and understandable diplomatic protest against the monstrously prejudiced ethnocentric defence he had put up.

4

— Westminster and its environs —

From the time when King Canute established his court near the ancient abbey, Thorney Island (the Westminster promontory turning the Thames) has housed England's administrative capital. The official royal presence still lies to its north in St James's Palace, shielded by St James's Park from immediate neighbourhood with the bureaucrats of Whitehall and the legislators of Parliament. In the vicinity of the palace, south of Piccadilly, many of the London gentlemen's clubs are to be found, and a couple of town mansions which are at the command of the royal family. A few diplomatic missions also lie hereabouts.

Not surprisingly, this is where prominent politicians have been assassinated: it was easy to find them here.

Spencer Perceval is the only British Prime Minister to have fallen to an assassin. But it was not his politics that killed him in 1812. John Bellingham nursed a private grievance. As a merchant in Russia he had fallen foul of the law and suffered imprisonment. His complaint to the British Ambassador, Lord Leverson-Gower, produced no diplomatic action, but annoyed the Russians who sentenced him to a second term. Bellingham was financially ruined, and on his release returned to London and petitioned for redress. He took shabby lodgings in New Millman Street, and sent addresses to politicians, civil servants, and even the Prince Regent. Each time he was politely but firmly brushed off. When the Prime Minister gave him similar treatment, Bellingham's self-control snapped. He took a pistol to the **House of Commons** and killed his 'tormentor' in the lobby.

Although it was clear that Bellingham had been unbalanced by his misfortunes, nobody thought him mad enough to justify reprieve at the time. Later he weighed on the conscience of lawyers, a fact which benefited Daniel Macnaughton (so spelled in his surviving autograph, though usually written 'M'Naghten').

In 1843 Macnaughton spent a week lurking around Whitehall. In the *Salopian Coffeehouse* **between Downing Street and Whitehall**, he shot Sir Robert Peel's secretary, William Drummond, probably because he thought Drummond was one of the hallucinatory 'persecutors' whom he believed were following him around and laughing at him. He variously identified these with 'the Jesuits', 'the Catholics', and 'the Tories'. The evidence of Macnaughton's longstanding paranoid hallucinations was so convincing and unrebutted by the prosecution that the judges stopped his trial and ordered his committal to Bedlam. Unfortunately the public and the Queen disliked this humane act, and the Law Lords were compelled to issue their alarmingly unscientific 'M'Naghten Rules', which reverted to an early eighteenth-century view that a madman was guilty of any crime he committed if he knew it to be wrong, instead of the more balanced view that a madman was not guilty if it was clear that his crime was the direct outcome of his madness.

The third and last political figure to be murdered in the heartland of politics was Airey Neave MP in 1979. The bomb placed in his car by the 'Irish National Liberation Army' was triggered to explode when tilted, and it did so as he drove onto the ramp from the **House of Commons** underground car park.

Near to Parliament Square, **Birdcage Walk** emerges from the south side of St James's Park. Here, in 1848, an unemployed housemaid named Annette Mayers shot Private Henry Ducker of the Coldstream Guards one fine spring morning. Ducker was stationed at the Wellington Barracks at the other end of the Walk, and Miss Mayers had bought the pistol deliberately in Regent Street (from James Beattie, whose gunsmith's shop was at no 205) with the intention of disentangling her love life. (She told Mr Beattie she wanted it to shoot a savage dog, and was embarrassed when he kindly offered to kill the brute for her. But gratefully regretting that she came from Hackney which would be too far for him to travel, she took the pistol.)

Ducker, it transpired, supplemented the Queen's shilling with monetary gifts from young ladies who fancied a uniformed lover. Annette could no longer disburse as she had no job, and she feared that he was receiving more than she could ever afford from another popsy who augmented her earnings by prostitution. She made no resistance to arrest, and denied nothing in court. But her sad story touched the Home Secretary and she was reprieved.

Petty France is a street running behind Wellington Barracks. South from it, narrow **Palmer Street** runs to Victoria Street. This lane once led to *Brewers Green*, when the district was still residential. Here yet another discharged housemaid committed murder. Elderly Elizabeth Mundell had taken pity on the young unemployed Martha Browning, and gave her shelter. Martha repaid this kindness by strangling the old lady with a rope and hastening her demise by suffocation, all for the sake of a £5 banknote.

What she did not know was that her booty was a forgery.

Mrs Mundell had detected it earlier, and shown it to her daughter Anne Gates. Instead of 'Bank of England', the words 'Bank of Engraving' appeared on it, and Mrs Gates recognized it as soon as she saw it in Martha's possession. Martha Browning was not reprieved.

North of the park, The Mall runs from Buckingham Palace to Admiralty Arch and, north again, **Pall Mall** runs parallel. A peaceful broad backwater of clubland today, it was more of an aristocratic jaunting-ground in the seventeenth and eighteenth centuries. Mr Thomas Thynne was killed in his coach at the southwest corner of the junction with today's Waterloo Place in 1681. Three thugs despatched him, and were duly caught, sentenced and hanged. But the real villain was Count Königsmark who had employed them. He envied Thynne's forthcoming marriage to heiress Lady Elizabeth Ogle, and hoped to win her himself by having his rival killed. Königsmark bribed the jury and avoided conviction.

In 1765 the *Star and Garter* tavern stood halfway down **Pall Mall**. Here Lord Byron, uncle of the poet, carried out one of those homicides that were almost an aristocrat's privilege. During the evening he quarrelled with his friend Mr Chaworth over the quantity of game on their respective estates. Fellow-drinkers assumed the quarrel was over by the time they all went home, but as the others went into the road, Byron pulled Chaworth back into a small room. Chaworth was run through by the noble lord's sword, but as his own had been drawn it could be argued that Byron had acted in self-defence. The House of Lords found Byron guilty of manslaughter, and Byron pled Benefit of Clergy: the ritual medieval survival which meant that a first offender who could read one verse of the Bible was declared to be under the jurisdiction of the church and released from punishment by the temporal courts.

In 1984 **St James's Square** witnessed a strange 'terrorist' assassination, by accredited diplomats whose accidental victim was a policewoman. The state of Libya under the adventurous leadership of Colonel Gadaffi made itself unpopular with the western powers by proclaiming both a socialist and an Islamic revolution. It seemed to provide a haven for all kinds of terrorist activity, and financed subversion abroad. More seriously, it exported its own counter-subversive activities, Libyans abroad being encouraged to strike down 'mad dogs' – or compatriots who opposed the regime.

In 1983 a group of young enthusiasts took over the Libyan People's Bureau at 5 St James's Square from calmer experienced diplomats. They were guided by a senior activist who was regarded as Gadaffi's chief hit-man in Europe. They aroused strong feelings among the Libyan community.

In April 1984 anti-Gadaffi Libyans planned a demonstration against the regime outside the People's Bureau. The diplomats and the Libyan government protested that they considered the toleration of such a demonstration an unfriendly action. Moreover they warned that counter-demonstrators would organize and they could not guarantee that the peace would be kept.

The police and the Home Office responded (with greater conviction than they offer to British demonstrators of the left and right extremes) that peaceful protest was constitutionally tolerated in Britain, and they would not be blackmailed into suppressing the anti-Gadaffyites.

When the demonstration took place, the police were marshalling the square to see that the rival factions were separated by crash barriers. But the threatened violence did not come from the street. To the astonishment of everyone in the square a burst of automatic gunfire came from a first-floor window in the embassy building itself. Several anti-Gadaffi demonstrators fell to the ground wounded. Police and civilians ducked for shelter. And WPC Yvonne Fletcher, who had been helping in crowd control, was left dead on the street.

Her colleagues recovered her body and sealed off the square. The embassy was kept under close siege for four days, while WPC Fletcher's hat lay in the gutter where it had rolled. The diplomatic status of the murderer or murderers meant that standard tactics of starving them out could not be followed. In the end, to the immense frustration of the police and public, the occupants of the People's Bureau had to be released and flown back to Libya. Diplomatic relations between the two countries were broken off. The Libyan government asserted that there was no evidence that the shots had come from the Bureau but were contradicted by all eye-witnesses. A memorial to WPC Fletcher was quickly erected in the square. The grotesque abuse of diplomatic privilege outraged the British government and people, and like all terrorist acts, was significantly counter-effective as a propaganda gesture.

East of Westminster, Pimlico and Victoria had a varied character. The prosperity of neighbouring Belgravia and Chelsea were not entirely shared by this sector of West London. Respectable working-class streets ran close to more comfortable bourgeois territory. Rather dismal office buildings sprang up in rather unexciting streets in Victoria. Charlwood Street in Pimlico was the home of Hetty Colquhoun, the prostitute who harboured the first suspect in the murder of taxi-driver Jacob Dickey, for which Alexander Mason (p. 206) was convicted.

This slightly transitory and undefined character is apparent in the district's most famous sudden death: the Pimlico Mystery as it was known in 1886. Adelaide Bartlett was an attractive, petite Anglo-Frenchwoman. Though she did not know it, she was probably the offspring of a French aristocrat and an English servant. She was brought up in France until she was eighteen when an English marriage was arranged for her.

Edwin Bartlett owned six groceries in South London. He had pretensions to gentility, for his first marital action was to send Adelaide to finishing school for three years. Once she was a fit chatelaine she settled down to domestic life in South London, first at Station Road, Herne Hill, and then at Lordship Lane, Dulwich Park. After that the Bartletts moved to Phipps Bridge Road, Merton, in a house that was, for once, not over a shop. And here they met the Rev George Dyson.

According to Dyson and Adelaide, Edwin was an eccentric who believed that a man should have two wives: one for company and one for pleasure. Adelaide claimed that she and Edwin had only once enjoyed sexual intercourse. When it led to a painful miscarriage, he agreed that they should completely forego any sex-life. Nobody was ever identified as Barlett's wife-for-pleasure, but the police found five condoms in his trouser pocket after his death, and the only book discovered in the Bartletts' flat was a Victorian sex manual.

But Edwin believed (according to Dyson and Adelaide) that his 'platonic' wife was entitled to a romantic attachment of her own. Although Dyson's cloth ruled out an adulterous liaison, it was with Mr Bartlett's entire approval that the young couple saw themselves engaged to marry should anything untoward happen to him, and exchanged affectionate kisses in his presence. Dyson even wrote execrable Victorian verses to 'My Birdie'.

At the end of 1885 the Bartletts moved to Pimlico, taking two first-floor rooms in *85* **Claverton Street** (the house no longer exists). Dyson, whose chapel was in Putney where he lodged at Parkfields, visited them. He also accepted a dubious commission from Adelaide, purchasing three bottles of chloroform from three different chemist's shops on December 28th. According to Adelaide it was wanted to relieve Edwin's pain from an unspecified internal complaint. But Dyson told the pharmacists (two of whom attended his chapel) that he proposed to use it for cleaning spots off clothes. And Adelaide claimed a third innocent use for the drug. Despite a painful jaw caused by incompetent dentistry, Edwin had recently attempted renewed conjugal sexual intercourse. Now this frightened her because of the suffering she had endured in her pregnancy; it was distasteful to her as a modest Victorian woman; and it was a terrible breach of faith with Dyson to whom she was 'betrothed'. So she kept the chloroform bottle beside her bed so that she could sprinkle a little on her handkerchief and wave it under her excited mate's nose to cool his ardour when necessary.

On New Year's Eve she sat up with him, holding his foot as he liked when suffering pain in his jaw. Early on New Year's morning she awoke to find that he had died in his sleep.

Edwin's father had never liked Adelaide, and was very suspicious of his son's unexpected death. An autopsy was carried out, and the stomach when opened reeked of chloroform.

Adelaide's story of her platonic marriage and approved engagement to George Dyson did not impress the authorities favourably. She found herself on trial, and Dyson was lucky not to appear in the dock beside her. As it was, Mr Justice Wills observed that Dyson appeared deplorably interested in saving his own skin. But then, the cynical judge had exploded the tale of the Bartletts' celibate marriage: the midwife, he elicited, had gathered that the intercourse leading to Adelaide's pregnancy was the only occasion on which Bartlett had not used his condoms with her!

For all his disapproval of the fancy-romance Adelaide presented as a modern marriage, the judge could not shake the crucial medical testimony in her favour. It was impossible to see how the chloroform could have been administered, since drinking it would have been agonizing and tissue in the mouth and throat would have been seared. Nobody could imagine little Mrs Bartlett rendering her husband unconscious and then forcing the liquid down his gullet. So although suicide and accident seemed equally improbable, the jury had to find Mrs Bartlett 'Not Guilty'. Public opinion was summed up in the alleged remark of a prominent surgeon, 'Now that it is all over, she should tell us, in the interests of science, how she did it.'

Claverton Street is at the southern end of Pimlico, leading to the river. **Tachbrook Street** is in the north, running from Victoria. A pedestrian precinct with a street market and a long block of postwar flats now dominates the upper end. But in 1928 there were ordinary houses, and a retired carpenter called William Holmyard lived at no 39. He had a short temper, and was annoyed when his grandson, an army bandsman also named William Holmyard, visited him to seek advice on getting a job. The old man cursed his namesake, and attacked him with a chair. Despite his age, he was stronger than the young soldier, who grabbed the tongs to defend himself, and hit him over the head. The blow cracked his grandfather's skull, and the old man died in hospital. For all the clear evidence that this was self-defence against a strong and unprovoked assailant, the lack of family piety shocked the court, and the unfortunate bandsman was hanged.

'Trunk murders' were briefly fashionable in the inter-war period. The most famous ones took place in Brighton. But in 1927 a trunk deposited in the left luggage office at Charing Cross station and uncollected aroused suspicion. Investigation exposed a woman's dismembered body wrapped in some clothes. No missing woman on police files fitted her description. An address on the trunk's label proved false, and the police were left with a small laundry mark on one garment as their only clue.

This led them to a Mrs Holt of Chelsea who identified the mark as one used for her servants' laundry. She thought the garments belonged to a Mrs Roles who had briefly worked for her as a cook.

A further police search turned up Mr Roles, who revealed that 'Mrs Roles' was not actually his wife, and their liaison had terminated some time previously. Her real husband, Roles thought, was an Italian waiter. Another cloth in the trunk led to the restaurant where the waiter worked, and Minnie Bonati was definitely identified. But neither Roles nor Bonati had any connection with her death.

A cab-driver was sure that he had taken a man with a trunk very like the one in question from **Rochester Row (off Victoria Street)** to Charing Cross. His pick-up point at *86* **Rochester Row**, almost opposite the police station, led to an abandoned third-floor office, whose tenant, John Robinson, had not been seen since the day when the trunk was deposited. The office was specklessly clean, and seemed an impossible site for a murder. Robinson might have been safe in his denial of all knowledge of Minnie Bonati, had not relentless police searching uncovered one bloodstained matchstick in a waste paper basket. This at last cracked Robinson's composure, and he told his story.

He claimed that Minnie had approached him on the street – begging, he averred, rather than soliciting. She had followed him to his office, and threatened him. In the resulting fracas he accidentally struck a blow which knocked her over so that she hit her head and killed herself. Then he panicked, rushed out to Staines' Kitchen Equipment Shop in Victoria Street and bought a knife with which to cut her up, packed her into the trunk and deposited her at Charing Cross.

His 'confession' came too late for his defence to seem convincing. Mr Robinson was hanged.

5

— Marylebone and Bloomsbury —

The village of St Mary-le-Bourne lay on the banks of Tyburn brook, southeast of the station which means 'Marylebone' to most people today. Marylebone High Street, east of Baker Street, runs south almost to Wigmore Street. Its suitability as a commuter town led to its merging with the old Tyburn Way (Oxford Street) and spreading east to Bloomsbury. Indeed, during the early nineteenth century the parish extended to Clerkenwell, so that places we now describe as 'Bloomsbury' might be described as 'Marylebone'.

Marylebone contained gracious town mansions, respectable petit bourgeois and artisan residential streets, and sordid slums. It now contains the only murder site distinguished by the GLC's blue historical marker plaque.

Cato Street lies two blocks east of the Edgware Road, between Crawford Place and Harrowby Street. Most of the street comprises desirable modern residences, but preserved at the Crawford Place end is the little building that was the site of the famous conspirators' arrest. In 1820 it was a disused barn with a loft above. Central London was full of cowkeepers who provided the capital's milk. When Mr Firth, who had kept three cows in Cato Street, retired he had an undesirable residence in a slummy backstreet at 'the west end of town' to let.

It had been empty for some time when the muddle-headed agitator Arthur Thistlewood rented it as a secret meeting place.

Thistlewood's twenty or so intimate supporters were all acquainted with dire poverty. They knew that there was no hope of social relief from the reactionary Tory government and decided on the wild gesture of assassinating the entire cabinet. At Cato Street they stockpiled guns, swords, homemade pikes and homemade hand-grenades. They knew that the cabinet were dining at Lord Harrowby's house in Grosvenor Square on February 22nd, and planned to take up positions outside the house, rush the first minister to leave as the door opened, throw hand-grenades into the hall, and use the confusion to burst in upon the rest of the cabinet and destroy them.

Typically, Thistlewood had no plan for constructive action to follow the murders. It sounded insane but, as the authorities wryly noted, the massacre might just have worked.

It was never attempted, because the conspirators were betrayed. A police spy warned the government and the dinner engagement was silently shifted to the Prime Minister's house. A magistrate with several constables and a small troop of soldiers raided Cato Street. Unfortunately, the soldiers went to the wrong end of the street, and the constables alone rushed the sentries and made their way up the barn ladder into the loft. Thistlewood recognized their leader as an agent who had previously arrested him, and fired a pistol which missed. Then with his sword he ran through the nearest constable, and fled to White Street, Little Moorfield, where he was again betrayed to arrest the following day. He was hanged and half-heartedly drawn and quartered along with five other conspirators.

A year later there was murder in the course of a robbery in one of the respectable parts of the parish. Dissatisfied

servants sometimes gave thieves inside information, and
Jane Robinson was dissatisfied. She did occasional cleaning
for widowed Mrs Lascelles of **Portman Square**, who also
employed a resident maid, 16-year-old Ann Ford, and
supported as a dependent her retired maid, 60-year-old
Elizabeth Green. Jane told James and Thomas Craig that
the house was worth robbing, described its lay-out, and
succeeded in hiding James inside the building, where he
waited for Mrs Lascelles and the maids to go to bed. At
2.00 A.M. he admitted his brother and Jane, together
with Mary Brown. Jane kept a look-out while the others
ransacked the house, strangled the old ladies and cut Ann
Ford's throat. Jane was caught trying to dispose of stolen
goods, and impeached the others after her own conviction.

In 1922 Henry Jacoby, an 18-year-old pantry boy, worked
at the *Spencer Hotel* in **Portman Street (near Marble Arch**.
The hotel is today the **Mostyn**, between Bryanston Street
and the Churchill). Widowed Lady White was one of the
hotel's residents, and her room was accessible to Jacoby
when he made up his mind to rob a guest. He left his
basement room in the middle of the night, took a hammer
from a workman's toolbag, and went a circuitous journey
through the kitchens to the guest rooms. Presumably Lady
White was disturbed, for he killed her with the hammer,
washed it carefully, and returned it to the toolbag and
himself to bed.

With the murder weapon successfully concealed the
crime presented problems. Nothing had been taken, and
there were no signs of a break-in. Jacoby attracted attention
to himself with an elaborate story of having heard 'voices'
when he went to the lavatory during the night. After a few
days' questioning he confessed.

The public was sympathetic. He was young. He was an
early claimant that violent movies had seduced him. He

was a 'poor' boy serving 'rich' guests. And, most seriously, he was in the public eye at the same time as Ronald True (p. 105). Since that revolting hearty had been reprieved, why should Jacoby hang?

The comparative judgment was ill-founded. The sole case for True's reprieve was the undoubted fact that he was mad as a hatter. Jacoby was not. Nor was he truly pathetic. His motives were immature and confused, but they were entirely selfish and, even if self-dramatizing, rational. His crime was the butchery of an old lady who had never done him any harm.

A few blocks north of the hotel is **Montagu Place** where Gordon Cummins (p. 65) committed his first murder. Three air raid shelters stood in the road in 1942, and it was in the central one of these that Cummins strangled 40-year-old schoolmistress Evelyn Hamilton, and stole her handbag.

In 1948 a professional thief snooping round the same area went into the basement flat at **75 Fursecroft, Bryanston Square**. As he was abstracting a wallet, Harry Lewis heard a voice, and realized that the occupant was getting out of bed and coming for him. Lewis hit him over the head with a chair and made his escape. Harry Michaelson, a 'lightning artist' who worked on the music-halls, died in hospital four days later. Lewis was hanged.

Flat 112 in **Bryanston Court** (turning into **Stourcliffe Street, off Bryanston Square**) saw an unusual tragedy in 1942. Twenty-year-old Derek Lees-Smith stabbed his mother. Unlike the infamous matricides Sidney Fox and Donald Merrett, Lees-Smith was not a psychopath. He suffered from hypoglycaemia, a blood-deficiency disease, which in his case led to confused episodes. It is assumed he

committed the murder during one of these, and he was
detained at His Majesty's pleasure.

John Tawell (p. 19) used Marylebone as the first
hideaway for his mistress Sarah Hadler. When she 'died
to the world' it was by moving to no 91 Crawford Street
next to the Duke of Wellington. Daniel Good (p. 223) left
his son with Jane Jones in the 'front kitchen' of 10 South
Street, Manchester Square (the eastern end of modern
Blandford Street) for the two years preceding her murder,
and hid there overnight after the police had discovered her
torso in Putney. Jane supported herself as a laundress. A
crude wooden board from her window reading 'Mangling
done Here' was produced at Good's trial for some reason.

The British Museum and London University gave an
intellectual heart to the district between Marylebone and
Clerkenwell. The clearance of the St Giles slums in the
latter half of the nineteenth century gave it respectability
though, like Marylebone itself, it had always been a region
of suddenly varying levels of prosperity.

Westward, between Tottenham Court Road and Cleveland Street, the area shared some of the cosmopolitan
bohemianism of Soho: eastward lay quiet squares and
comfortable residential streets. In the early nineteenth
century, before the museum and the university had spread
across opposite sides of **Montague Place**, this road was
similar to the others around. Number 11 was owned by a
Mr Lett of Dulwich, who kept it as an occasional town
residence, leaving a Mrs Jeffe as housekeeper to look after
it. A young ne'er-do-well named William Jones was a
family friend of Mr Lett, and through him became
acquainted with Mrs Jeffe. The housekeeper felt sorry for
the young man and gave him money when he was unable
to make ends meet. Jones took advantage of the fact that
she was normally alone to cut her throat and rob her.

The Russell Hotel, where Russell Square adjoins Southampton Row, has twice given hospitality to murderers and their ladies. In 1966 Harry Roberts (p. 148) passed the night after the massacre in Braybrook Street here with Mrs Lillian Perry, before disappearing with his camping gear in the direction of Epping Forest. And forty years earlier, bearded Frenchman Pierre Vaquier stayed here with Mrs Alfred Jones, landlady of the Blue Anchor Hotel, Byfleet, Sussex. Despite an almost total language barrier, their physical relations proved so satisfactory that Vaquier made immediate plans to eliminate Mr Jones by poison. It was at the chemist's shop in 134 Southampton Row that he bought strychnine, claiming he needed it for wireless experiments, and delighting all future generations by signing the poisons book as 'Mr Wanker'. Jones was poisoned in Sussex, and Vaquier, much to his surprise and indignation, was easily detected and convicted.

The western side of Tottenham Court Road has a more murderous reputation. Louis Voisin, a Belgian butcher, lived in the basement at *101* **Charlotte Street**. (The end of the street has been rebuilt, but to the south the older residential style of housing survives.) He was evidently attractive to ladies of his own nationality. Mme Emilienne Gerard, who lived half a mile north of him in Munster Square came to his apartment one night in 1917 seeking shelter from a threatened air raid. There she found that she had been supplanted in his affections. Berthe Roche was now actually living with Voisin.

The ladies quarrelled and came to blows. Voisin intervened. And somehow he and Roche battered Mme Gerard to death.

Voisin promptly used professional expertise to dismember her. Her torso was swaddled in her beribboned lace underwear and thrust in a sack; her legs more simply

packed in brown paper. On the paper, to suggest a xenophobic antiwar motive, Voisin wrote 'Bloody Belgium' –
only he spelt it 'Blodie Belgiam'. Then he loaded his
parcels on to his cart and drove them across Bloomsbury
to Regent Square, between Gray's Inn Road and Judd
Street, where he dumped them behind the railings.

They were found the next morning. Voisin was easily
traced once Mme Gerard's underwear had been identified.
His false clue served only to trap him when he repeated
the mis-spelling at the request of the police. And a search
of his basement kitchen revealed not only copious human
bloodstains, but also, thrust away in a gloomy little arched
recess, Mme Gerard's head and hands preserved in a
barrel of alum. Voisin was hanged, and Berthe Roche did
not long survive her imprisonment.

A little way down the street at Jay's jeweller's shop (no
73–5) Charles Jenkins, younger brother of Thomas (p.
23) continued the undesirable family tradition of violent
robbery. With his two friends Christopher Geraghty and
Terence Rolt he carried out a smash and grab raid in
1947. A motor-cyclist named Alec De Antiquis tried to
stop the young hoodlums from escaping down Tottenham
Street into Tottenham Court Road. They shot him, and
ran to change their outer clothes in Brook House, 191
Tottenham Court Road. 'Fabian of the Yard' traced them
through the scarf and raincoat Jenkins abandoned there,
and the two older boys were hanged: Rolt, a seventeen-
year-old, was detained at His Majesty's pleasure.

At the other end of Charlotte Street, no 18 is still a
continental delicatessen, and still claims neighbourhood
with Fitzroy Square by calling itself the Fitzroy Stores. In
1911 the grocery business was owned by the happily named
Mr Barnett Rotto, who also allowed the upstairs part of
the premises to be used as a house of assignation. It was

here that Steinie Morrison (p. 43) brought Jane Brodsky for her sixteenth birthday seduction – a treat she enjoyed so much that she tried to repay him with an inadequately prepared false alibi at his trial for murder.

Actual prostitution flourished in the region of **Grafton Way** (then Grafton Street) in the nineteenth century. In 1845 Thomas Hocker (p. 111) came blithely here to tell one girlfriend a cock-and-bull story of having torn his sleeve while 'romping' with another immediately after he had in fact murdered James De la Rue. In 1894 Marie Hermann, an old lady who had long passed suitability for her profession, battered a 70-year-old cab driver to death in her first-floor flat at no 51. The next day she hurried off to new digs at 56 Upper Marylebone Street, taking with her a heavy trunk. Blood in a common sink at Grafton Street led to a search of her flat, and the discovery of more bloodstains. A search of the trunk revealed the body. Marie was lucky. The young Marshall Hall defended her, and made his name with this, the first case in which he satisfied a jury that his female client had accidentally killed her victim in self-defence.

Whitfield Street runs off Grafton Way. Doris Piernecke, another elderly prostitute (of Polish origin) was found in bed here with her throat cut in 1903. The coroner's jury returned an open verdict, as it was just possible that she might have committed suicide.

6

—— Fashionable West London ——

Lying between Oxford Street and Piccadilly, Mayfair developed almost as a continuation of Marylebone parish. But it lacked the slum pockets that disfigured its northern neighbour, and was well situated to become the fashionable residential 'West End of town'. Expensive shops spread from New Bond Street; embassies established themselves, and large blocks of luxury mansion flats replaced town houses at the western end near Hyde Park.

South of the park, nineteenth-century prosperity gave rise to still grander town houses. Belgravia was an eastward extension of fashionable Chelsea from Sloane Street. Its residential interior has never been taken over by shopkeepers: Harrods in Knightsbridge is still within easy walking distance from any part. Here again, diplomatic legations established themselves among the homes of the very rich.

The upper-class character of the two districts is reflected in their patterns of murder. Despite a centre of street prostitution around Shepherd Market, these gracious streets have never been disfigured by mutilated bodies. Apart from an incursion by Patrick Mackay (p. 99) who learned to prey on rich elderly women in Chelsea, the casual street robber has not victimised the wealthy residents and threatened their lives. Instead, these two districts remained the last outposts of that common pre-industrial phenomenon, murder involving domestic servants.

One of the worst eighteenth-century servant murders took place in **Bruton Street** (between Berkeley Square and New Bond Street). In 1769 Sarah Metyard, a milliner, subjected her maid Ann Naylor to the cruel and unusual punishment of tying her hands to her bedroom doorknob so that the poor girl could neither sit nor lie down. She was left there for three days without food, at the end of which time she died. Helped by her daughter, Mrs Metyard packed the body into a box and kept it in her garret for two months. By then it was becoming inconvenient, so the two women dismembered it, and carried the pieces across town to Chick Lane in Farringdon, where they strewed them in the open drains.

They were not identified as human, and the murder would never have been suspected had not mother and daughter quarrelled four years later. Fearful of her mother's anger, Miss Metyard fled the house and took refuge with friends to whom she confessed the reason for her terror. The shocked friends told the authorities, and Miss Metyard's confession did not save her from sharing her mother's fate on the gallows.

Society was perturbed by the murder of Lord William Russell in 1840. The ageing aristocrat was a somewhat tetchy employer, but it was not his temper which led his Swiss valet, François Courvoisier to kill him. Courvoisier was a thief who had already secreted some of the household silver with a compatriot at the Dieppe Hotel, Leicester Place. His position was deservedly endangered, and Courvoisier decided to murder his master and take whatever further property he fancied. Mindful of the risk of bloodstains, he stripped naked in the middle of the night, and crept to Lord William's bedroom in the house at *14 Norfolk Street* (today's **Dunraven Street**, parallel with the north end of Park Lane) where he cut the old man's throat with

his own razor. In the morning he pretended amazement
when his master was discovered lifeless in his bloodsoaked
sheets.

Number 14 no longer exists, but many Mayfair houses
still exhibit graceful ornamental fanlights over their front
doors. Through one of these a neighbour is said to have
observed the strange sight of a naked man creeping down
the stairs with a candle in the dead of night.

It was obvious to the police that this was an inside job.
Courvoisier was hanged, to the great satisfaction of the
servant-employing classes, who could hardly have been
more shocked if an armchair had turned assassin.

Another lethal foreign servant – this time one whose
mistreatment by her employer won her sympathy and a
reprieve – was Marguerite Diblanc, a Belgian.

Her mistress was a top-bracket kept woman named
Madame Riel, who lived at **13 Park Lane**. Her rent was
paid by Lord Lucan, the Crimean War general who ordered
the Light Brigade to charge.

In 1872 Madame Riel dismissed her maid with a month's
notice, but only a week's wages. This high-handed behaviour incensed Marguerite, who strangled the lady with her
bare hands and dragged her by a rope around her neck
from the open cellar where the deed was done to a more
secluded pantry. She then helped herself to money and
jewels, and fled to France.

The French police found her, and she was returned to
England for trial, sentence, reprieve and imprisonment.

For some reason, Belgravia has seen markedly more murders than Mayfair. Indeed, the very first execution of
Queen Victoria's reign, in 1837, resulted from goings-on at
21 Cadogan Place (off Sloane Street close to Knightsbridge, and arguably part of Chelsea). Unusually, a servant

murdered a servant: 18-year-old William Marchant cut the throat of equally young Elizabeth Paynton. He seemed to have hoped for a little hanky-panky below stairs and turned nasty when she resisted. He pleaded guilty, but there were no mitigating circumstances.

A sillier servant-boy was Ernest Albert Walker, 17-year-old footman to Colonel Trotter of **Lowndes Square**. While his employer was away, Walker amused himself by sending for a messenger boy from the Sloane Street Messenger Service. When young Raymond Davis arrived, Walker took him down to the basement, hit him over the head and tied him up. As his victim recovered consciousness, Walker proceeded to inflict simple tortures on him, ending his idiotic and wicked entertainment by opening a gas-tap which he apparently intended to kill the pair of them.

Davis died, but Walker revived. Unnerved by his adventure he ran away, but gave himself up to the police in Tonbridge. He was fortunate that in 1922 he was too young to hang.

A few blocks south in the same year Field Marshal Sir Henry Wilson, Chief of the Imperial General Staff during World War I, was gunned down on the front doorstep of **36 Eaton Place** as he returned home in dress uniform from unveiling the Euston war memorial. With that heroic recourse to outdated military measures which had characterized the profession of arms in Britain for decades, Sir Henry gallantly drew his ceremonial sword in self-defence.

The assassins, Reginald Dunn and Joseph O'Sullivan, commandeered a taxi and a victoria before backing away on foot to Ebury Street firing at pursuers and injuring two policemen, before they were caught and nearly lynched. 'Politically' motivated Irish murderers were as unpopular in 1922 as they are today.

Mrs Elvira Dolores Barney enjoyed a sensational trial in 1932 after her 24-year-old-lover, Scott Stephen, had been found shot through the chest at point-blank range on the stairs of her home, **21 William Mews**. A divorcee three years older than Stephen, Mrs Barney was a fairly representative 'bright young thing'. Her neighbours were accustomed to hearing frenzied quarrels. Mrs Barney had been seen threatening Stephen with her pistol, and heard threatening to take her own life. On the night of May 31st they went out to the Café de Paris. They came home drunk; a typical quarrel ensued; and, behold, Stephen was dead.

Mrs Barney claimed it had been an accident. She had, she said, intended to turn the pistol on herself, and it went off as Stephen tried to stop her. She took refuge with her parents, around the corner in Belgrave Square, and they engaged elegant, gentlemanly Patrick Hastings to defend her. He persuaded the jury the pistol's trigger spring was lighter than expert gunsmiths averred, and Mrs Barney was acquitted. Contrasting her idle-rich fate with that of the self-supporting but otherwise curiously similar Ruth Ellis (p. 158) one concludes that there is one law for the bitch and another for the whore.

A plaque at the eastern end of **Chester Square** commemorates the presence of Queen Wilhelmina of the Netherlands' staff-in-exile during the war years. At the other end of the same square, at no 45 in the shadow of the church, another exiled monarch lived: King George of Greece. He did not spend all his time in Chester Square, and on a flying visit to the house in 1946, he remained unaware that his housekeeper's body lay where it had been shot on the premises.

Elizabeth MacLindon was engaged to a man named Arthur Boyce. She did not know that Boyce was already married, and furthermore had been convicted of bigamy.

Bigamists make dangerous lovers. Boyce decided to break off the entanglement violently when she was alone in the house. He shot her with a Browning revolver he had stolen from a former room-mate, and left her body where it lay, to be undiscovered for a week. To allay suspicion, he wrote to her from Brighton asking why she did not answer the telephone when he called.

But the bullet in Miss MacLindon was shown to match a spent cartridge fired by Boyce's former room-mate. The revolver was never found but the shabby deceiver was trapped.

The last servant-murder in Belgravia was surely intended to be a wife-murder. Richard John Bingham, seventh Earl of Lucan, brought new and undesirable celebrity to his ancient name in 1974. His subsequent disappearance added to his notoriety. And the coroner's jury that brought in a verdict of murder against him, even though he had not (and has not) been discovered, dismayed his few friends who still hoped that he was alive and capable of providing an innocent explanation.

'Lucky' Lucan was an unsuccessful professional gambler. At the time of his disappearance he was heavily overdrawn, and unable to gain further credit at the bank or to raise money from usurers. He had separated from his attractive wife, and grievously missed his small children, to whom he was immensely attached. Lady Lucan and the children retained the comfortable house at **6 Lower Belgrave Street**, while Lucan took up residence in the mews behind them at 5 Eaton Row. It was easy for him to walk round to the house and look up at the windows, or down through the area at the basement. And this he claimed he had done on the night when Sandra Rivett, the children's nanny, died.

According to Lucan, he was casually passing, and

noticed a strange man fighting with a woman in the basement. He let himself in with his key, but the man rushed out past him, leaving Miss Rivett dead in the basement, where Lady Lucan found both of them when she came down to see why the nanny was taking so long to make a cup of tea.

Yet very soon, Lady Lucan herself was to burst into the Plumbers Arms, a pub a little way south of no 46, hysterically insisting that 'a man' had broken into the house, killed Sandra and attacked her. It would seem that this man must have been Lord Lucan.

Under normal circumstances Sandra Rivett would have been out for her night off. The assumption made by the coroner's jury was that Lucan, knowing this, hid in the house intending to kill Lady Lucan, bundle her into a sack and transport her body in the boot of his car to an unknown destination. He would then recover custody of his children and the full use of his house. The plan misfired because Miss Rivett had not gone out and was killed by mistake. Lucan's quick impromptu story of the intruder was told over the telephone to his mother and repeated to friends with whom he stayed overnight. His car was later found near Newhaven. Lord Lucan has not been seen since, and despite reported overseas 'sightings' it seems probable that he committed suicide.

Chelsea enjoys a long history as a village upstream of Westminster and London. Charles II loved the route to Hampton Court through its demesnes. By the late nineteenth century it became a favoured residential area for artists and intellectuals.

At the same time, extensive newer developments of upper-middle-class housing stretched north and west to fill the space between Sloane Street and Hyde Park: Dickens's 'Stucconia' of the nouveau-riche.

An early incident in *'Chelsea Fields'*, near the manor house **(Chelsea Manor Gardens** today: streets rather than pleasure-grounds) demonstrated the fine line between socially acceptable duelling and criminal violence. In 1705 Edward Jefferies was walking with Elizabeth Torshall in a path from the mulberry garden to the house when he spotted Robert Woodcock approaching. Jefferies told Elizabeth to walk ahead while he had a word with the stranger. He rejoined Elizabeth alone, and told her he had quarrelled and fought with Woodcock, and had 'given him a prick' – perfectly gentlemanly conduct. But the boys who found Woodcock's body discovered that the dead man had been killed with his own sword, and Jefferies was proved to have taken his money. Despite Elizabeth Torshall's attempts to support his story he was hanged.

Sixty years later the territory was still rural. In 1771 Levy Weil, a failed immigrant doctor who had taken to robbery in London, his brother Asher, Jacob Lazarus and Solomon Porter went through Five Fields (west of Sloane Square and along the **King's Road**, to the farmhouse of Mrs Hutchings. They broke in and tied the lady up with her petticoats over her head. While they were ransacking the house, the hired hands John Slow and William Stone woke up and intervened. Stone was killed in the fight, and the four robbers were executed after having been anathematized by their synagogue.

The intelligentsia and the rising bourgeoisie are relatively unmurderous groups. Nineteenth-century Chelsea and 'Stucconia' were not marked by much violence. But the presence of unprotected elderly people living on private incomes has attracted some unpleasant predators in the twentieth century.

John George Haigh was the most infamous of these. In 1949 he lived in the Onslow Court Hotel at the south end of Queen's Gate where it runs into Old Brompton Road. He passed as a businessman and inventor. Just around the corner at **79 Gloucester Road** he rented the basement (still highly visible from the road) as a workshop. In September 1944 he had used this workshop to dispose of a young amusement arcade operator named William Donald McSwan whom he had known for some years. When McSwan brought a pintable in for repair, Haigh coshed him, and dissolved his body in a water-butt filled with acid.

McSwan's parents were also acquaintances. Haigh told them their son had gone into hiding from his call-up. In July 1945 Haigh used the basement to kill both of them, just as he had their son, and carried out the most successful coup of a fifteen-year career in fraud and forgery. Passing himself off as young McSwan he gave himself power of attorney over the parents' property, sold four houses and cashed a large quantity of securities, netting at least £4000 (a substantial sum in 1945).

By 1947 he had gambled it away. He inveigled his way into friendship with Dr and Mrs Archibald Henderson by pretending an interest in buying their attractive terrace house at 22 Ladbroke Square. He remained their friend as they moved to 16 Dawes Road, Fulham, and visited them when they went to stay in a Brighton hotel in February 1948.

By now Haigh had the use of a less overlooked workroom. A light-engineering firm in Crawley, Sussex, loaned him a rarely used store room. He lured the Hendersons there, shot them, and dissolved their bodies in acid baths. Forged documents transferred their car and house to Haigh. Together with jewellery and personal possessions, he netted nearly £8000 from this murder. Yet he dissipated the lot in less than a year and once more found himself pressed for funds.

His appearance was dapper; his manners charming. To the elderly ladies who were permanent residents at the Onslow Court the youthful entrepreneur seemed a delightful and interesting companion. In search of new pickings he turned his attentions and charm on Mrs Olive Durand-Deacon, a rich widow whose dining-table adjoined his. He discussed the manufacture of artificial finger-nails with her – it seems to have been her idea – and invited her to inspect his workshop in Crawley. There he shot her through the head, removed her portable jewellery and persian lamb coat, and destroyed her body with several carboys of sulphuric acid which he had bought for his 'business'.

But Mrs Durand-Deacon's disappearance worried another elderly lady in the hotel, and Haigh's assumed anxiety and voluntary journey to inform the police could not lift suspicion from him.

By the time the trip to the Crawley workshop was investigated, all that remained of the unfortunate lady was her false teeth, some fragments of bone, and a plastic handbag. Chemical analysis proved that the sludge tipped from Haigh's acid vat contained a high proportion of dissolved animal fat. The persian lamb coat and jewellery were produced by a cleaner and jeweller respectively: they had received them from Haigh. He had been seen in Crawley with this victim. The horrible charmer was arrested.

He damaged his subsequent defence by immediately asking the police what chance they felt anyone had of being released from Broadmoor. There seemed little reason to doubt that he was making a calculated attempt to save his neck when he confessed to his earlier murders, adding three unlikely and unproven non-financial killings with the dramatic claim that he felt an impulse to kill because he

needed to drink his victims' blood. Haigh's descriptions of
his madness seemed more indebted to Bram Stoker than to
any homicidal compulsions recognized by psychopath-
ology. Although revulsion against capital punishment was
growing in the 1940s, and most executions aroused some
protest, Haigh died universally unlamented.

Gunther Fritz Podola had not been in England long in
1959 when he robbed some flats in Roland House, Roland
Gardens and followed the robbery with a clumsy attempt
at blackmail. He telephoned a Mrs Schiffman, falsely
claiming to have found discreditable material in the burglary of her flat and trying to extort money from her.
Having nothing to fear, Mrs Schiffman agreed to receive
another telephone call from him, and informed the police.
Thus her telephone was being monitored when Podola
called again from a public box in South Kensington's
elegant glass-roofed underground station, and Mrs Schiffman kept him on the line until the police had surrounded
him.

Podola broke away from arrest, crossed the branch of
Onslow Square facing the underground station, and ran
along the Square proper in the direction of Onslow Gardens. At the end of the square he raced up the steps of no
105, a large house converted into apartments with a very
broad front entrance. From a hiding place behind the
pillars in the hall he shot Detective Sergeant Raymond
Purdy, and made his getaway in the ensuing confusion.

Within a few days Podola was traced to a cheap hotel
just around the corner from the scene of the crime – no 95
Queen's Gate (which now houses an organization whose
signs are all hand-written in Arabic). It took some courage
for the police to break into the room of this armed and
dangerous murderer. They broke the door down and
charged in a rush. Podola emerged with a black eye and

some bruising. Police claims that he had been struck by the door as it burst open were widely doubted: it seemed quite plausible that the arresting officers might have beaten up their colleague's murderer. But this paled into insignificance compared with Podola's claim that the shock had caused him a total loss of memory.

The court had two problems to resolve. As a question of fact was Podola's amnesia genuine? As a question of law, was he fit to plead and stand trial if he genuinely had no recollection whatsoever of the crime? In the event, the courts found against Podola who was convicted and hanged. In retrospect, the protests surrounding his particular case seem a little contrived. There was no question whatsoever that Podola had murdered Sergeant Purdy, and it could hardly be acceptable law that a subsequent illness should constitute a valid defence.

The third of the evil predators to batten on the defenceless old ladies of the Royal Borough was a multiple murderer who certainly killed in Gravesend, claimed to have killed on Hungerford Bridge, seems circumstantially likely to have killed in Finsbury Park, and is strongly suspected of murders in New Cross, Kentish Town, Hertfordshire, Hackney and Southend. But since two of the murders for which Patrick Mackay was brought to book took place in the Chelsea or Sloane Street region, this roving death threat may well be dealt with here.

Born in South London in 1952, Mackay was the son of an alcoholic clerk who habitually battered his family. With this experience of upbringing the boy's ultimate derangement is hardly surprising, although some writers on Patrick Mackay have unobtrusively hinted at his mixed racial parentage (his mother was Guyanese). Actually the heritage Guyana bequeaths its children is a marked and often solicitous charm. This characteristic would be useful to the tall and good-looking Mackay in winning his victims' confidence.

By 1973 Mackay was beyond his mother's control and had begun his short career of restless wanderings around accommodation addresses, friends' houses and hostels. In July he was staying with an aunt in Catford when a 17-year-old au-pair girl named Heidi Mnilk was stabbed in the throat on a train from London Bridge. Her killer left the train at New Cross, and Mackay is suspected.

In the same month 73-year-old Mary Hynes was found battered to death in her flat in **Kentish Town**. The file on the case indicates police satisfaction that Mackay was the murderer.

By his own confession, Mackay fell into one of his periodic lightning rages when he encountered an old tramp on **Hungerford footbridge** in January 1974. He threw the man into the Thames, but since no body has been recovered and no suitable missing vagrant identified, the murder is not officially recognized.

Around this time Mackay found work in Hertfordshire. Furniture-loading first took him to Mrs Stephanie Britton's house at Hadley Green. On January 12th he was employed as a groundsman about a mile away when an intruder stabbed Mrs Britton and her 14-year-old grandson Christopher Martin. Mackay has denied the murders, but strong suspicion attaches to him.

Isabella Griffiths was an 84-year-old widow living at **19 Cheyne Walk**, the fine row of houses facing the river. Mackay won her good opinion by running errands for her. On St Valentine's Day he terminated their friendship forcefully by throttling and stabbing her.

Mackay had also been befriended by Fr Anthony Crean, a Catholic priest from Gravesend who tried hard to rescue him from his hopeless descent into drifting and petty crime. (Fr Crean was, of course, unaware of Mackay's major crimes.) At the same time, Mackay had discovered that mugging old ladies was an easy way for a fit young man, 6ft 4 inches tall, to keep himself in petty cash.

This did not inhibit him from ordinary robbery. He confessed to breaking into Frank Goodman's tobacconist's shop in **Rock Street, Finsbury Park** and robbing the till on June 13th. He conceded that a bloodstained footprint in the shop was his, and led the police to a cemetery where he had discarded his boots. But he denied responsibility for battering the old shopkeeper to death with a lead pipe.

On December 23rd, while Mackay was living in a hostel on the Great North Road beyond Archway, somebody followed 92-year-old Sarah Rodwell from the Temple Street Tap in Hackney (on the edge of Bethnal Green – now a trendy black-walled and mirrored wine bar) to her flat nearby in Ash Grove (the flats are demolished, but the walk through dark canalside lanes from Temple Street to **Ash Grove** is impressive). She was battered to death on her doorstep, and her £5 Christmas bonus was stolen. Mackay is suspected.

In February 1975 Ivy Davies was killed at her home in Southend-on-Sea by an axe-blow. Mackay admitted that he was very familiar with her Orange Tree Café, and had been considering robbing it.

On March 10th 89-year-old Adele Price was returning to her third-floor flat in **Lowndes Square**, when she encountered a tall young man on the pavement searching for his keys with the apparent intention of letting himself in. She admitted him, and sympathetically invited him into her flat when he complained of faintness and asked for a glass of water. Once in the privacy of her kitchen, Mackay stabbed her. Then, uncharacteristically, he claimed to have tried to kill himself.

His career was moving to its close. Friends in Grantham Road, Stockwell, with whom he was staying teased him about Fr Crean's friendship. They suggested that the priest's only real interest in Mackay was homosexual. Outraged at being put in a humiliating position and unable to solve such a problem except by violence, Mackay hurried away to Gravesend where, on March 21st, he felled his benefactor with an axe, and then watched him drown in his increasingly bloodstained bath.

This murder was too close to home. Mackay was an obviously suspicious acquaintance of the dead man, and his apprehension gave the police the melancholy satisfaction of clearing up a very large number of far-flung murders over the previous two years.

Roy Fontaine (born Archibald Hall) was a predator before he came to Chelsea. He had made himself into a first-class butler or 'gentleman's gentleman', and wrote his own glowing references to conceal his criminal record. Fontaine, in fact, impersonated his employers, stole from them and forged their signatures. He was a solid professional criminal who regarded an employer as a live-in mark, and felt himself to be enjoying a holiday if he accepted a post without intending to rob his boss.

A prison boyfriend came up to join him on one of his 'holiday' contracts, looking after a rich widow's house in Scotland. The boyfriend refused to accept the propriety of living in wealthy surroundings without felonious purpose; demanded that Fontaine rob the house or be exposed, and finally shot at him (and missed) as the butler lay in bed. Fontaine had to get rid of this nightmare associate. He took him 'rabbit-shooting', and returned alone. The body was buried cunningly in the bed of a stream, and Fontaine had got away with murder.

1977 found Fontaine working at flat 22, **Richmond Court, Sloane Street**, the home of retired Labour MP Walter Scott-Elliot, and his handsome Anglo-Indian wife

Dorothy. Both were extremely rich, and Fontaine devised a complicated plan to manoeuvre their property into his own hands. To this end he needed an accomplice. Mary Coggle, an old girlfriend (Fontaine was bisexual), introduced him to a petty South London crook on the run, Michael Kitto. The meeting took place in the Lancelot pub, Baker Street, and proved satisfactory. Fontaine showed Kitto round the flat when Mrs Scott-Elliot had supposedly been taken to hospital, so both men were acutely surprised when the lady emerged from her bedroom having been discharged early. With unadmirable presence of mind they suffocated her with a pillow. A disturbed Mr Scott-Elliot was easily reassured that his wife had woken with a nightmare, and their excellent Jeeves had settled her down again.

The next job was the disposal of the body and taking care of Walter. The old man was obviously on the verge of senility, and Fontaine rightly anticipated that doping him with tranquillisers and sedatives would reduce him from a danger to an inconvenience. Scotland having hidden the first victim so satisfactorily, the second was destined for a trip north. Fontaine and Kitto hired a car and put her in the boot. Then they procured a wig for Mary Coggle and persuaded her to pass herself off to Walter as his wife. Astonishingly, this worked! The sedated ex-legislator looked puzzled at her unlikely hair from time to time, but never actually questioned the identity of this complete stranger who purported to be his wife of thirty years and had solecistic notions of how the upper crust speak.

The preposterous motoring party reached the Highlands, where Dorothy was buried. Walter was found to be an impediment and was also killed and buried. Mary Coggle also became an impediment when she insisted that she wanted to keep Dorothy's fur coats, instead of accepting that the gang would make more money by realizing securities and covering their traces. So she too was killed and buried. Finally Fontaine killed his younger brother Donald, mainly because he had never liked him.

Before Donald could be buried the car was stopped in a routine police check and, like Peter Sutcliffe the Yorkshire Ripper, Fontaine found himself required to explain why he was using false number-plates. Dreading having to explain why his hired car had his brother's body in the boot, Fontaine did not wait for the questions to begin. His attempt at flight was folly. He was caught, exposed and convicted.

Countess Teresa Lubienska, an elderly Polish lady with a heroic war record, was living in Cornwall Gardens in 1957. One day she staggered, bleeding, into the lift at **Gloucester Road tube station**, moaning, 'Bandits! Bandits!' She died of stab wounds before reaching hospital. The old lady used the term 'bandits' for the ill-mannered, and it is assumed that she imperiously reproved some unknown young delinquents who responded with deplorable violence.

Madar Lal Dhingra's murder of Sir Curzon Wyllie in 1909 occurred in Kensington simply because the *Imperial Institute* (now absorbed in **Imperial College of Science and Technology**) happened to lie between the Albert Hall and the Natural Science Museum. This shooting at a public concert was a straightforward political assassination. Dhingra was an anti-imperialist Indian nationalist and Wyllie the treasurer of the National Indian Association, a charity in whose aid the concert was being given.

Thomas Ley and John Smith were known as 'the chalk-pit murderers' in 1946, because their victim's body was found in a chalkpit at Woldingham. The actual murder took

–

place in **5 Beaufort Gardens**, between Brompton Road and Pont Street. The house belonged to Ley, an Australian who had once been Minister of Justice for New South Wales. Smith was one of the workmen employed to convert it to flats. He and his fellow labourer John Buckingham were assigned the additional task of helping Ley torture, kill and dispose of John Mudie, a barman of the Reigate Hotel. Ley told them Maudie was a blackmailer – a complete fiction.

In fact, Ley was suffering from severe paranoid delusions. He had lived at 16 Knightsbridge Court, Sloane Street, with a Mrs Brooke, until she went to Wimbledon to look after her son-in-law. There she lodged in the same house as Mudie, 3 Homefield Road, and Ley imagined the two to be lovers. This illusory jealousy led him to plot the murder. He was unpleasantly domineering and calculating, but quite sick enough to justify the reprieve which he did not long survive.

As the borders of Earls Court and Fulham are reached, the confident upper-middle-class prosperity of Brompton and Chelsea steadily yields to seedier flatland. Today **Finborough Road** carries northbound traffic from Kings Road to Earl's Court. In the 1920s and '40s it was a rather drab residential backwater. Its three-storey terrace houses have prominent basement areas, sometimes arched over by airy bridges of steps to the front doors. Two of these basements at the Fulham end of the road were prominent murder sites.

The first and more important was the basement flat at **no 13.** Here, in 1922, a lady named Gertrude Yates – professionally known as Olive Young – made her living by entertaining gentlemen callers. Most unfortunately for her, one of these was the superficially dashing ne'er-do-well, Ronald True.

Miss Young did not welcome True as a client. On his first visit to her he had stolen £5 so, without drawing attention to her occupation by making a fuss, she discreetly tried to discourage his requests for another visit. But True was not to be deterred by tact, and called repeatedly at the flat until the fateful night when he found her in again, and she agreed to let him stay.

To casual acquaintances, True exhibited the hearty hilarity that passed for middle-class charm in the age of Sapper and Dornford Yates. To those who knew him better, he was a dismal disaster. Alcoholic, drug-addicted, psychopathically dishonest and hopelessly unable to hold down a steady job, True never found it possible to adjust to the expectations and demands imposed by his middle-class upbringing and his decent education at Bedford Grammar School. He failed as a colonial farmer and a Canadian mountie: he was a wartime disaster in the RFC. The unfortunate American girl who married him soon realized that he was a hopeless mental case.

When True met Miss Young he was moving from hotel to hotel leaving unpaid bills behind him; borrowing and stealing small sums from acquaintances; dishonestly leading the leisured life he found appropriate to his accent, clothes and style.

Miss Young entertained her clients overnight, and so her maid, Emily Steel, coming in from down the road at no 61 to clean up in the morning, was not surprised to receive a hearty greeting from a well-dressed gentleman who asserted that he had left Miss Young drinking her cup of tea in bed, where she didn't want to be disturbed yet. True took himself breezily off to pawn some jewellery he had extracted from Miss Young's dressing-table. He then met a new acquaintance named James Armstrong in Fulham, hired a car to take them both down to Croydon for tea, and returned to the Hammersmith Palace of Varieties for the evening performance, where he was arrested.

For Emily Steel had found that the motionless shape huddled in Miss Young's bedclothes was nothing but a pair of bloodstained pillows. Miss Young's naked battered body had been dragged into the bathroom. (True actually *had* made her morning tea and taken it to her bedside, however.)

True's insouciant failure to cover his tracks at all suggested madness. His 'defence' – a claim that a look-alike, strangely named 'Ronald *Trew*' had been going around London committing the frauds of which he was accused, and had probably committed the murder – was intrinsically insane. There was copious evidence that anyone who had worked with him had thought he was mad. Only the legal confusion of the McNaghten rules and True's own insufferable personality could really have led anyone seeing his trial to imagine that he could be hanged. But the coincidence that Henry Jacoby (p. 82) was convicted at the same time (and was considerably startled by a hearty invitation from fellow-prisoner True to 'Come and join our Murderers' Club!') led to some protests against his reprieve. Some people thought True's class background had won him the privilege of reprieve: as though a toff could kill a tart and live, while a boot-boy who murdered a lady must die. In fact Broadmoor was the right place for True, whose back-slapping extraversion found a useful niche as leader of its inmates' entertainments committee until his death in the 1950s.

At **17 Finborough Road**, just two doors away from the scene of Miss Young's death, a widowed engineer called Cyril Epton used a hammer and a flat-iron to batter Winifred Mulholland to death in 1946. Then, recognizing the potential usefulness of the narrow wrought-iron balcony running along the first floors of the terrace, and the deep basement area, with a dangerous parapet shielding the steps down, he hurled the body into the area, hoping the injuries would be ascribed to an accidental fall. Forensic science exposed the ruse and Epton was convicted.

7

——— North of Marylebone ———

The northward suburban sprawl from Marylebone was
broken by the salvaging of Regent's Park and Primrose
Hill from the fields where Londoners had historically
enjoyed holiday walks. Streets of attractive villas grew up
around the park, and to the northwest comfortable Victorian suburbs developed through St John's Wood and Swiss
Cottage, reaching out to Hampstead.

While this land was all still countryside, England's
most consequential political murder gained permanent
association with Primrose Hill. In the reign of Charles II,
Sir Edmund Berry Godfrey, coal merchant and magistrate,
was a prominent citizen, living at Hartshorn Lane off
Northumberland Street, where the Thames' bank then lay
– 500ft further inland than it does today.

In 1687 Dr Israel Tong, a crackpot Presbyterian clergy-
man, and Titus Oates, an unfrocked priest, managed to
have papers propounding Tong's theory that the Papists
were planning a regicide brought to Charles's attention.
Sir Edmund Godfrey, as a reliable magistrate, was desig-
nated to take depositions from Oates and Tong.

Soon after examining the 'informers' Godfrey appeared
to fear for his life, and on October 12th, after walking to
the fields in the north and making enquiries as to the
whereabouts of Paddington Woods, he disappeared.

Immediately highly circumstantial rumours began to fly
around town that he had been kidnapped and murdered

by the Papists, and on October 17th his body was found in a ditch on *Greenberry Hill*. This rise is today's **Barrow Hill**, at the southwest corner of Primrose Hill, with a reservoir at its crest and a couple of blocks of flats on its southern slope.

Godfrey had been strangled – probably with his own cravat, which was missing – and run through with his own sword. His badly bruised chest showed that he had been beaten. It was rumoured that he had been killed in town, and this has not been seriously challenged since. But the claim of two informers named Captain Bedloe and Miles Prance that the murder had been carried out by the Duchess of York's Catholic servants in her residence at Somerset House has been rejected by all subsequent historians.

On Bedloe and Prance's contradictory evidence, three Catholics named Berry, Green and Hill were arrested, tried and hanged, despite the fact that they all had excellent alibis. The trial was conducted by the notorious Chief Justice Scroggs, with his still more infamous successor, Jeffreys, prosecuting. These two turned the trial into a parody of justice, hectoring and bullying the defendants. The ignorant populace noted that the defendants' names joined to form the 'murder' site – 'Green-Berry-Hill' – and concluded that Providence had predetermined their exposure.

But the serious outcome of the murder and trial was that Oates, Tong and their allies were able to represent Godfrey's murder as the first blow in the Catholic conspiracy to kill England's rulers. The authorities failed to check the notorious witch-hunt known as 'the Popish plot', and the country became prey to unscrupulous informers.

Godfrey's murder has been mysterious for years. It was never clear who stood to gain by his death and it is only recently that Stephen Knight's excellent research uncovered the fact that Godfrey was himself a member of a secret faction of Protestant extremists linked with Oates and Tong. Knight noted that the Duchess of York's Catholic secretary fled after the questioning of Oates and Tong, but before its results were made public, and made the plausible suggestion that Godfrey had warned this personal friend of danger. If it appeared to the heads of the conspiracy that he was leaking, then, as Godfrey well knew, they would stop at nothing to prevent him from betraying them.

Knight even proposed a candidate for the actual murderer: the psychopathic bigot Philip Herbert, Earl of Pembroke. But, as he recognized, he was far from proving Herbert's complicity: he established only that Herbert had the convictions, temperament, habits and opportunity to have undertaken the deed, and that one contemporary rumour placed the killing in Leicester Fields where Herbert had a house.

Another murder in the fields has been misrepresented over the last hundred and forty years because of the murderer's romantic fantasies and the peculiar means he used to lure his victim to a spot **half a mile north of Primrose Hill**.

Thomas Hocker and James De La Rue, aged 22 and 27 respectively, were a pair of randy young Victorian bucks. They affected sprigged waistcoats and collected pornographic prints. They had an extensive female acquaintance among servant girls and near-prostitutes. But since neither intended to be bound by marriage or paternity suits, they used false names in their dealings with them.

There was one important difference between the two. De La Rue earned enough as a piano teacher to support himself comfortably in lodgings at 55 Whittlebury Street (off Drummond Street, which then led into Euston Square). Hocker barely made ends meet by giving occasional violin lessons, though he was convinced that he was unusually

talented and deserved a comfortable living. He was the son
of a poor shoemaker, and shared a bedroom with his
brother at 11 Victoria Place, close to their father's home, 17
Charles Street, Portland Town (today's Charlbert Street).

On February 23rd 1845 a passing policeman heard cries
of 'murder' coming from the bridle path through the fields
between Primrose Hill and Belsize Park. Beside the old
wall of *Belsize Park* (roughly **where Primrose Hill Road
and Englands Lane meet Belsize Park Gardens** today)
he found the battered body of De La Rue. His watch and
money were missing. But he carried a letter in pretty blue
ink and a girlish hand addressed to 'J. Cooper'. In it,
'Caroline' coyly warned 'Dear James' that she was pregnant and requested a meeting at their unspecified usual
place. The policeman blew his whistle and awaited help.

Twenty minutes later it arrived in the form of Hocker,
loping across the fields from the Swiss Cottage tavern. He
gave no sign of recognizing the deceased 'Mr Cooper', but
patronizingly confirmed that he was dead and hung around
for nearly half an hour before other assistance turned up.
Then he took his leave, and went cheerfully on to Grafton
Street (today's Grafton Way, off Tottenham Court Road)
where two of his lady friends lived. The publicity given the
case was to prove highly embarrassing for them: the older
sister of one discovered for the first time that she had been
sharing Hocker's affections, and the other who worked as a
maid for Sir Oswald Moseley lost her job when it transpired
that she had exploited her employers' absence from their
house in Osnaburgh Street to let Hocker and friends 'romp'
in the bedrooms.

When De La Rue was identified, Hocker's family was
surprised by his impassivity on learning that his best friend
had been found murdered under an assumed name. De La
Rue's watch was found in his possession. His brother and
a lady friend confirmed that the 'Dear James' letter was

ABOVE: Elizabeth Brownrigg, hanged in 1766 for causing the death of a maid by her cruelty

BELOW: Artist's impression of Mrs Brownrigg inflicting punishment

LEFT: Buck's Row, where Jack the Ripper's first definite victim, Polly Nichols, was found. (At the time she was thought to be the third)

BELOW: Mitre Square before modern renovations. Catherine Eddowes, second victim on the night of Jack the Ripper's double killing was found in this corner

LEFT: Miller's Court off Dorset Street. Mary Kelly, the Ripper's final victim, was last seen alive at this entry

RIGHT: 29 Hanbury Street. Jack the Ripper and Annie Chapman crept through the street door and out to the backyard without waking the seventeen people sleeping in the house

The Kray twins leaving the Stoke Newington flats where they lived while they ruled the East End underworld. The author now lives in the same block

The Blind Beggar in Whitechapel Road. Headquarters of a nineteenth century gang of hoodlums, and scene of Ronald Kray's murder of George Cornell

Henry Jacoby, boot-boy who battered a hotel resident

Stage door of the Adelphi Theatre. The ornamented door at the right (originally leading to the royal box) was used by William Terriss as his private entry when he was stabbed by 'Mad Archie' Prince

ABOVE: The hotel where John George Haigh lived and met his final victim, Mrs Olive Durand-Deacon
BELOW: Ronald True in the dock

RIGHT: Lord Lucan's house where Sandra Rivett was killed in the basement

BELOW: In 1820 this was a disused cowshed in Cato Street where revolutionary conspirators met in the loft and their leader stabbed a constable sent in the party to arrest them

OPPOSITE ABOVE: Ruth Ellis, the last woman hanged in England

OPPOSITE BELOW: Ruth Ellis shot David Blakeley in this street outside The Magdala Tavern in Hampstead

LEFT: Dr Crippen

BELOW: Crippen's house, 39 Hilldrop Crescent, second from the left. The building was destroyed during the war

ABOVE: 10 Rillington Place. The ground floor flat became Christie's mausoleum for four victims, including his wife

LEFT: The squalid garden of 10 Rillington Place, where Christie buried his first two victims

Reg Christie, affecting pride in his gardening

195 Melrose Avenue, where Dennis Nilsen rented the ground floor flat and buried twelve victims in the back garden between 1979 and 1981

ABOVE: Nilsen being taken from court after his conviction

RIGHT: 23 Cranley Gardens, where Nilsen blocked the drains with the flesh of his last three victims

LEFT: Joe Orton, brilliant playwright murdered by his jealous lover

RIGHT: The house in Noel Road, Islington, where Orton shared a flat with Kenneth Halliwell, who killed them both

RIGHT: Brian Donald Hume, spiv and murderer

LEFT: 620 Finchley Road, where Hume killed Stanley Setty in the upstairs flat

ABOVE LEFT: Charles Bravo, victim of mysterious tartar emetic poisoning

ABOVE RIGHT: Florence Bravo, twice bereaved of husbands who happened to have taken tartar emetic

LEFT: Front door of The Priory, the Bravos' expensive house on the edge of Tooting Bec Common

THE PRIORY
225

written in one of several false hands that Hocker often assumed, and the unusual blue ink was traced to his room. The winter had been unbrokenly frosty since mid-December, and Hocker had worn two pairs of trousers and a pair of knee-length drawers against the cold on the night of the murder. All three garments were found to be blood-soaked at the knees. Hocker was arrested.

Hocker pretended that chivalrous reasons inhibited him from explaining what had really happened. He claimed that he had knelt in a pool of blood in an abattoir to stain his trousers and distract suspicion from another person. His prolific fantasies have left an erroneous impression that Hocker and De La Rue quarrelled over a romantic attachment. Actually, Hocker's crime was the mean murder of his best friend for petty gain. The only romance in his life consisted of more or less squalid liaisons. He was a vain and silly psychopath.

Five years earlier, a crime occurred between Hampstead Road and Albany Street, east of the Park, which was recalled by the press throughout the 1840s whenever the police had difficulty in tracing a murderer. The *King's Arms Wine Vaults* stood between De La Rue's lodgings and Sir Oswald Moseley's misused town house at what was then the corner of *Brooke Street* with *Frederick Street* off the Hampstead Road (roughly where **Longford Street joins Osnaburgh Place** today). Eliza Davis started work there when she was thirteen. By 1837, when she was twenty-one, she had risen to barmaid and was well-liked by her employers and customers. They were dismayed when she was found one morning, lying behind the bar with her throat cut.

There had been no sexual assault and there was no indication of any struggle. There had been no robbery.

It was recalled that she had recently refused to serve a

Frenchman called Emtré who had then threatened her. Emtré was not to be found. The landlord suspected a gipsy-like man he had seen hanging around the bar, and was convinced that he returned several years later. But no one was ever charged with the crime.

Avenue Road runs from Swiss Cottage alongside Primrose Hill to Regent's Park. In 1949 a 3-year-old girl called Marion Ward was killed here by Mrs Nora Tierney, who dumped the body on a bomb-site at **Langham Court**. She was committed to Broadmoor for the crime – which had been witnessed by her own little daughter. And while investigating, the police found the battered body of a vagrant called Reginald Short in the grounds. His murder was never solved.

Mrs Alice Middleton, the wife of a merchant navy officer, was in the habit of taking lodgings while her husband was at sea. In 1922 she lodged with a tailor named Cecil Maltby, who lived over his shop at *24* **Park Road**. A new construction of flats and shops now covers the site, though rather run-down shops a few blocks to the north suggest the street's interwar commercial character.

Maltby inherited his father's business but failed in it. Bankrupt and separated from his wife and children, he was sinking into alcoholic despair when Mrs Middleton came to live with him. At some point in August, probably while drunk, he shot Mrs Middleton and put her body in the bath. Then he went completely to pieces.

He barricaded himself into the house, and refused to come out although his water, gas and electricity were cut off. The neighbours saw the premises becoming squalid and insanitary, and complained to the authorities. But there were no grounds for the police to enter until in

January a sanitary inspector obtained a warrant to investigate. The police then broke in, and as they did so, Maltby shot himself.

They found the building appallingly filthy. But the most horrible evidence of Maltby's total breakdown was the bath. This still contained Mrs Middleton's body, but it had been boarded over, and Maltby had used it as a dining-table during his months of self-confinement.

A murderer who recovered or retained his awareness of reality was Adam Ogilvie. The body of Mrs Olive Nixon was found, in 1946, lying beside a garden wall in **Park Village East**, a most attractive street of individualized late nineteenth-century houses overlooking a wall which secludes the railway line to the east of the park. Her head had been battered with a brick. Manic assaults on lone women by strangers are the hardest form of murder to solve, and it was not surprising that the police did not detect the culprit. But ten years later Ogilvie confessed. He had made one further attack on a woman after Mrs Nixon's death, but as it was in faraway Torquay nobody had connected the two incidents. Now in 1956 he felt the urge to murder coming over him again and, with exceptional good sense, gave himself up to the police.

The construction of 'The New North Road between Paddington and Islington' led to a rash of building along its route. Subsequently great railway termini lined it, and we should today think of the areas traversed as Marylebone, Euston, St Pancras and King's Cross. But before the 1850s, these regions were more likely to be thought of as Hampstead Road, Portland Town, Somers Town, Brill and Battle Bridge: decent artisans' suburbs with occasional 'shy' areas where policing was unwelcome.

In Brill, Esther Hibner of **13 Pratt Terrace**, St Pancras Road (today's **Pratt Street, Camden Town**) ran a tambour-working business with her daughter, Esther junior, and a forewoman, Ann Robinson. Six workhouse orphans were apprenticed to her.

The little girls slept on one blanket with no bed. They had one slice of bread for breakfast with a quarter-pint of milk between them. Every other Sunday they had a slice of meat. For the rest of their food they shared nine pounds of potatoes a week. The notorious workhouse diets were generous in comparison.

The children worked from 3.30 A.M. until 11.00 P.M. daily, and were caned almost hourly for slacking. One named Frances Colpitts was punished by being held by her heels and dipped headfirst into a bucket of water by Esther junior, while Ann Robinson screamed, 'Damn her! Dip her again and finish her!'

After this Frances took sick, and the Hibners fobbed off her grandmother, who tried to visit her, saying that she had 'been naughty' and was not allowed visitors. The suspicious grandmother reported the matter to the parish, and the beadle came on a tour of inspection. He was horrified to find the children lousy, ragged and starving. Frances had abcesses on the lungs, and within a few days died in the workhouse infirmary.

The Hibners and Robinson were put on trial in February 1829, but the judge had to warn the jury that they could not convict all three of murder. If they found that the 'dipping' had directly caused the child's death they could convict Esther junior and Ann Robinson: if they felt that the general malnutrition and ill-treatment had killed her, they must blame the elder Hibner. The jury chose the latter course. Esther was hanged, and her partners were remanded to prison to await further charges.

In 1907 railway chef Bertram Shaw rented upstairs lodgings at *29 St Paul's Road* (now **Agar Grove**). He went to
Sheffield daily on the evening train and returned the
following morning. On September 12th he found his sitting-
room ransacked and his wife locked in the bedroom with
her throat cut.

Phyllis Dimmock was not really Mrs Bert Shaw,
although she so described herself. Shaw's occupation made
it convenient for her to pursue hers during his nightly
absence; she was a popular local prostitute, picking men
up in nearby pubs (especially The Rising Sun at the corner
of Euston Road and Chalton Street). On the three nights
before her death, she had taken a ship's cook home with
her. But she had refused to make an appointment for the
fourth, showing him a letter, part of which read:

> Dear Phillis,
> Will you meet me at the bar of the *Eagle* at
> Camden Town, 8.30 tonight, Wednesday.
> Bert

and a postcard which read:

> Phillis Darling.
> If it pleases you meet me at *8.15* P.M. at the
> [*Rising Sun*]
> Yours to a cinder
> Alice

Instead of the words 'Rising Sun', there was an effective
little sketch showing a red-nosed sun beaming and winking
over the horizon.

Despite the different signatures, both letter and card
were written in the same hand. The charred letter was
found in Phyllis's fireplace; the postcard a few days later.
The cook had an impeccable alibi for the Wednesday night;
Mr Shaw was not the Bert who had written the letter;

Phyllis had been seen in The Eagle with a young man who had often accompanied her during previous weeks; so the hunt was on for the creator of the postcard.

When it was published in the newspapers a pretty prostitute named Ruby Young recognized it as the work of a young graphic artist named Robert Wood, who lived in St Pancras, and had graduated from client to boyfriend of hers and then, a few months previously, dropped her. Ruby, good-natured and attached to Wood, agreed to cover for him and refrained from claiming the £100 reward for information offered by the *News of the World*. But she told a friend . . . who told a friend . . . and Wood was arrested and identified by several witnesses as having been with Phyllis Dimmock in The Eagle on the night she died, and subsequently leaving 29 St Paul's Road at dawn.

He was extremely lucky that the circumstantial evidence against him was confined to his seeming to be the last person to have seen Phyllis before her murder. One blood-stain on his clothing must surely have hanged him. But he made a surprisingly good impression in the witness-box and was acquitted.

29 Agar Grove is a bare brick box of a semi-detached, with a shallow-pitched roof and nine steps up to a square porticoed front door: a shabby example of bedsitland. Agar Grove leads through Randolph Street into Royal College Street almost opposite the saloon bar entrance to The Eagle where Phyllis spent her last evening with Wood. The exterior of The Rising Sun, two blocks east of Euston station on Chalton Street, is a wonderful late Victorian extravaganza. Inside, red pillars with Corinthian capitals support a heavily embossed ceiling, whose fleur-de-lys pattern is relieved by a smiling sun at the door. Wood's sun was appropriately more raffish.

One other murder attracted a little attention in Camden Town. In 1933 a garden shed at *30* **Hawley Crescent** (where TV-AM's industrial funfair architecture now covers the road) burnt down one night. Inside was found a charred body and a suicide note from the unsuccessful businessman who had rented the shed for use as an office. But the suspicious circumstance that the body was still seated at the desk led to the discovery that it was actually the remains of a rent collector named Walter Spatchett, and not the 'suicide', Samuel Furnace. Furnace was arrested in Southend, and successfully killed himself while in custody.

Westward across Kentish Town Road and Camden Street, Bonny Street gives access to sinister Prowse Place under the railway arch, and secluded **Ivor Street** (formerly *Priory Street*) leading from it. In October 1890 neighbours saw Mrs Mary Eleanor Pearcey pushing a top-heavily loaded pram covered with American cloth under the arch after dark.

Mrs Pearcey went for a six-mile walk with the pram and came home without it. She headed west to Chalk Farm and then northward to the half-built Crossfield Road, where she dumped her heaviest bundle: the body of 31-year-old Phoebe Hogg. A long walk north up the Finchley Road at length brought her to Cock and Hoop Field, at the junction of West End Lane with Cannon Hill. Here she dumped Phoebe's baby who had been smothered under the weight of her mother's body. Then she struck south down West End Lane to Maida Vale, and veered into Hamilton Terrace, where the much abused perambulator collapsed and was left outside no 34. And at last Mrs Pearcey went home.

Mrs Pearcey was not really Mrs Pearcey, but Miss Wheeler. Since the age of sixteen she had been living off men: first a labourer called Pearcey who kept her in Camden Town for two years and whose name she adopted. He gave her up when she started an affair with furniture

remover Thomas Hogg, who lived at 141 Prince of Wales
Road, between Kentish Town Road and Haverstock Hill.

Hogg could not afford to support her, and soon married
Phoebe who was expecting his baby. So a Gravesend
'gentleman of independent means' named Charles Crichton
became her keeper. He rented the ground-floor apartment
of *2 Priory Street* for her, furnished it attractively with a
piano, and visited her at his own convenience for sexual
relief.

She, for her pleasure, gave Hogg a duplicate key to her
house, and enjoyed his twice-weekly visits for sex. Her
relations with Phoebe were satisfactory until Phoebe fell ill
over Christmas 1889; on her recovery visits between the
two ceased. This estrangement seems to have preyed on
Eleanor's none-too-strong mind, and in October she wrote
a note inviting Phoebe to tea, and spied from the corner of
Crogsland Road as the messenger boy delivered it. The
tea-party obviously went badly, as Mrs Pearcey struck Mrs
Hogg over the head with a poker and cut her throat before
taking her and the baby out for a long walk.

When the police came the next day she vaguely ascribed
the bloodstains in her kitchen to 'killing mice', and sat at
the piano humming in a pretence of ignoring their questions. She seemed unhinged by her infatuation for Hogg.
She never realized that killing his baby daughter affected
the way he felt about her, and distantly 'forgave' him for
not easing her last days before her execution with a
sympathetic visit.

Mrs Pearcey's house and Mrs Hogg's still stand. The
murder has been associated with Hampstead and with
Kentish Town, but the fatal kitchen was in Camden Town.

The various 'North London' murders of the first decades of
the twentieth century took place in the suburbs north of

Camden Town, Pentonville and Islington. The brick terraces and semis of Holloway, Highbury and Finsbury Park testified to the spread of the reputable clerical classes: murder was especially shocking in this region. Crippen and Seddon lived here, with 'Brides-in-the-Bath' Smith only a little farther north in Highate.

Hawley Harvey Crippen is one of the great names of English crime. For fifty years after his arrest he was *the* classic murderer in most English eyes.

It was the contrast between his respectable, genteel exterior and his grisly secret that made Crippen so interesting. For five months in 1910 he lived placidly in *39* **Hilldrop Crescent** (between Camden Road and Hilldrop Road, next to the Brecknock Road crossing), going to work daily at Albion House, New Oxford Street, where he partnered a fellow-American in a dentistry practice and acted as agent for the patent medicine firm which had originally brought him to London.

And at night he returned to sleep peacefully in Hilldrop Crescent where, as he knew, the bricks of the cellar floor covered quantities of flesh carved off the body of his late wife, Cora (or 'Belle Elmore' as she called herself in a mediocre music-hall career), wrapped in one of his old pyjama jackets. Since the flesh was packed in lime, Crippen assumed it would be destroyed rapidly: but he had added water and had thereby *preserved* it. When dug up and examined by the police after five months interment the remains were found to contain hyoscine, a poison Crippen had bought in unusually large quantities a week before his wife was last seen alive. And the remains also included a horseshoe-shaped piece of skin, fringed with recognizable pubic hair and marked with an operation scar. From this, Mrs Crippen could be positively identified: she had had an ovarectomy a few years previously.

Mrs Crippen's acquaintance were suspicious of the doctor's explanations for his wife's disappearance. *Prima facie* there was no reason why an American's American wife should not have been recalled suddenly to the sickbed of a relative in the USA, there taken ill herself, and died, even if the developing story had an air of improvisation. But it was intriguing that the husband should have moved his young secretary in to live with him immediately. And it was positively suspicious that Ethel Le Neve should be seen abroad in Mrs Crippen's clothes and jewels. Mrs Crippen's friends were dissatisfied and made their own enquiries. With great difficulty they persuaded the police to take an interest. At last, in July, Inspector Walter Dew was despatched to Hilldrop Crescent to 'shake up' the doctor.

It is well known that Crippen only gave himself away by his panic and subsequent flight on being questioned by Dew. His instant admission that the story of Belle's death in America was false and had only been made up to conceal his embarrassment at having been cuckolded and deserted convinced the good inspector, and led to his being sharply criticized when Belle's remains were discovered. But a glance at Hilldrop Crescent today explains easily why the well dressed, bespectacled little doctor made a good impression.

Number 39 no longer stands; it was destroyed by a bomb during the war and has been replaced by a block of council flats. But the surrounding three-storeyed semis are imposing, if a little close together. The crescent is still quiet, and breathes respectability.

Once Crippen had fled and the police were able to examine his house the squalor underneath came to view. Like many another murderer demoralized by his crime, Crippen had taken to passing most of his life in one room, the basement kitchen, which had become a sordid jumble of dirty dishes and soiled clothes. His financial affairs were less secure than they seemed. Belle had taken at least two other lovers in England: an American one-man-band performer from the music-halls, and a German student who had temporarily lodged with the Crippens at Hilldrop Crescent. Crippen and Ethel had made furtive afternoon assignations in the cheap hotels of Argyle Square, King's Cross.

Ethel's disguise as a boy; the couple's flight for America as Mr and Master Robinson on the *Montrose*; Captain Kendall's suspicion of his passengers, his quite extraordinary snooping on them and their luggage, and his historic marconigram to Scotland Yard; Inspector Dew's pursuit on the faster *Laurentic* and arrest of Crippen in Quebec: these are all familiar. British newspaper coverage of Crippen during the week at sea made him the household word he was to remain: Captain Kendall enjoyed using his wireless to keep the public informed, and he even transformed Ethel from the romantic to the comic companion of the runaway monster murderer when he revealed that her trousers had started to split at the back, and were fastened with a safety pin.

How and when Crippen administered hyoscine to Cora is not known; nor do we know when and where he cut her up, or how he disposed of her bones and head. His guilt was never doubted from the time of his flight until the suggestion, many years later, that he bought the hyoscine as an anaphrodisiac to blunt Belle's supposedly voracious sexual appetite and misjudged the dose. So it is worth pointing out that the Crippens' motive in taking a short lease on 39 Hilldrop Crescent (they had previously lived in flats on Store Street off Tottenham Court Road) was to give themselves separate bedrooms. Judging by her lovers, Belle's tastes had run to father figures when she was nineteen and had married Crippen (her second older man).

And ten years later she preferred a more vigorous virility to Crippen's gentleness: her one-man-band player was an ex-pugilist with a wife and children in Chicago; her German was hearty and jocular.

There can be little doubt that Crippen killed his wife because she was in the way. His devoted love letters to Ethel show that he was determined to lay his masochistic soul at the foot of his new woman (and so probably turn her into another shrew). He did not protest his innocence after the trial. And Ethel was extremely lucky to be tried separately as an accessory after the fact and acquitted.

North of Seven Sisters Road between Stroud Green Road and Hornsey Road runs Tollington Park, broad, long, straight and lined with capacious, desirable houses for the late-Victorian rising petit bourgeoisie. The houses are built in blocks and short terraces, three storeys high, with large additional basements, and a variety of brick patterns to ornament them. The road is a clear cut above its offshoots of terraced cottages and the less individualised houses on the main roads flanking it.

Frederick Seddon, area supervisor for an industrial insurance company, prospered by thrift, calculation and hard work. In his wife's name he ran a secondhand clothes business at 276 Seven Sisters Road – a glance at the drab brick floors above the newsagent on the site today suggests the dull life 'over the shop' Seddon lived in 1909 – and he invested his savings in mortgaged house property which he regularly sold profitably. After one successful sale, he bought **63 Tollington Park** as an investment and quickly realized that he could advantageously move his large family (wife, five children and elderly father) into the fourteen-room speculation and still let parts of it. He moved his office from the shop in Seven Sisters Road, charged his own employers rent for the basement room where he kept their takings in a safe, and took tenants for the four rooms on the top floor.

Miss Eliza Barrow, a 49-year-old valetudinarian spinster with private property to the tune of £4000, had made herself responsible for the orphaned children of a former landlady in Clapton. An adolescent girl named Hilda was at boarding school, and a little boy of 9 or 10 years old named Ernie Grant lived with Miss Barrow in a quick succession of lodgings, culminating for fifteen months at her cousins', the Frank Vonderahes', in 31 Evershot Road. The house was confined – one of the small terraces running off Tollington Park, just two blocks away from no 63 – and tension soon developed. On one occasion Miss Barrow spat at Mrs Vonderahe. In 1910 Miss Barrow and Ernie moved into the four-room top-floor flat of Seddon's new house.

According to Seddon, Miss Barrow was worried about her investments after Lloyd George's famous budget of 1909. He made some quick calculations and agreed to take over her properties in Camden Town (a seventeen-year lease on the small Buck's Head pub in Camden High Street and the tiny adjoining building *1* Buck Street which was then a barber's shop) in return for a small annuity and the remission of her rent. Early in 1911 he increased the annuity in exchange for her India Stock.

Over the next few weeks, Mrs Seddon exchanged thirty £5 notes in local shops. These were shown by their numbers to have been Miss Barrow's, and Mrs Seddon was never able to give a satisfactory explanation for having endorsed them with the fictitious name 'Mrs Scott' of 10 or 18 Evershot Road.

In the summer of 1911 Miss Barrow fell violently and nauseatingly ill, with constant diarrhoea and vomiting. To Seddon's disgust she insisted that Ernie sleep with her. The top floor of the house stank so badly that the doctor advised the Seddons to hang sheets soaked in carbolic around the sickroom.

Within two weeks, after several disturbed nights, Miss Barrow's heart failed and she died.

Seddon arranged for an undertaker to give her the cheapest possible burial in a public grave, and accepted a commission for introducing the business. The Vonderahes were later to claim that this was scandalous, as there was room in a family vault for Miss Barrow's respectable interment; but neither they nor the authorities transferred her body there after its exhumation made that possible.

It was the Vonderahes who brought about Seddon's downfall, when they belatedly learned of Miss Barrow's death, and felt that Seddon was unduly obstructive when they tried to find out what property she had left. They insisted on an exhumation, and arsenic was found in Miss Barrow's body. Some very dubious evidence averred that Maggie Seddon had purchased arsenic flypapers from a Mr Thorley, whose chemist's shop was at 27 Crouch Hill (now the site of a Marler's Bar). Sir Bernard Spilsbury conceded that apart from the surprisingly well preserved state of Miss Barrow's remains her internal organs showed all the symptoms of death by the natural cause alleged on her death certificate. Marshall Hall, appearing for Seddon, did his best to persuade the jury of the unreliability of the tests for quantities of arsenic made by Professor Willcox. But Seddon was doomed by his confident, calculating and aggressive performance in the witness box.

A surprisingly large public petition failed to secure his reprieve, and Filson Young's introduction to the *Notable Trials* volume on the Seddons hints at his suspicion of a possible miscarriage of justice. It is clear that the unfortunate and suggestible Miss Barrow was surrounded by relatives who were passionately interested in her money and hated the more successful *rentier* who had profited by their comparatively rich cousin. But the general classy fastidiousness which has persistently despised Seddon and his lodger as misers pays too little attention to their demonstrated willingness to support the orphaned Ernie Grant as long as either could; to Seddon's attempts to arrange to take over caring for Hilda before his arrest; and to Ernie's unforced testimony that, unlike the Vonderahes, 'Chickie' (as he called Miss Barrow) and the Seddons were always very kind to him.

Ronald Marwood's stabbing of PC Raymond Summers on the pavement outside Eugene Grey's Dance Academy at *133* **Seven Sisters Road** in 1958 (toward the Holloway end, and now demolished) was the outcome of a brawl among young men which might have happened in any city. But Marwood and his friends were ordinary working lads, not young tearaways like the East End gangs who had been scrapping to their hearts' content for generations. And so the police intervened, and Marwood, carried away by the excitement, stabbed Constable Summers who was arresting his best friend. The boys all fled at once. Marwood's success in hiding out for a month (with friends at Chalk Farm) gave his name a national prominence it would not otherwise have merited, as did the fact that killing a policeman in the execution of his duty placed him in one of the few categories then liable to be hanged for murder.

8

—————— West London ——————

The little village of Paddington developed as a dormitory suburb during the nineteenth century. Its famous green dwindled away as more houses were built. The Great Western Railway terminus lowered the character of the neighbourhood and some residents moved north into Maida Vale, where good quality terraced villas were built (to be replaced by comfortable but characterless mansion flats during the twentieth century).

John Tawell (p. 19) briefly housed the unfortunate Sarah Hadler in Paddington, north of the green where the Harrow Road runs to Harrow Road Bridge today. James Greenacre (p. 202) dumped Hannah Brown's torso behind a flagstone leaning against the garden wall of the newly built Cambridge Villas at Pineapple Place in the Edgware Road (on the west side of Maida Vale between Elgin Avenue and Sutherland Avenue in 1835, now replaced by modern flats). Since this was the first part of Miss Brown to be discovered, Greenacre's crime was usually referred to as the 'Edgware Road' or 'Pineapple Toll-gate' murder.

Gordon Cummins (p. 65) draws attention to prostitution in the sub-standard housing and short-stay hotels south of Praed Street. He picked up his victims in the West End, but strangled and mutilated Doris Jouannet at her flat in **187 Sussex Gardens**, and attacked Kathleen King or Mulcahy in hers at 29 Southwick Street.

The A6 murder is the most famous crime with strong Paddington connections. In the late summer of 1961 Michael Gregsten and Valery Storey were parked in a field near Slough, when a strange man approached their car, held them up at gunpoint and forced them to spend the night driving around the northwestern outskirts of London. It was a complete shock to Miss Storey when, with dawn approaching, the man suddenly shot Gregsten through the head in a lay-by on the A6 and raped her. He then forced her out of the car and fired several more shots at her, driving away awkwardly when convinced that she was dead.

Miss Storey was in fact alive, though paralysed from the waist down. The assault and murder horrified the country. There was widespread concern that the unknown villain should be brought to book. The police took Peter Louis Alphon in for questioning after hearing that he had paced up and down his hotel room near Finsbury Park for five nights after the murder.

This strange loner denied all involvement, but was unable to prove an alibi. He was released when Miss Storey not only failed to recognize him in an identity parade, but positively identified another man who was unquestionably innocent.

The murder weapon was discovered hidden under the upstairs back seat of a London bus, and soon the police were questioning a young burglar named James Hanratty, who was known to have recommended this as a hiding-place for unwanted swag. Hanratty foolishly put forward a false alibi. Like fellow-burglar Steinie Morrison (p. 43) he automatically tried to hide his movements from the police, and the exposure of his lies in court put his life in jeopardy. Miss Storey identified Hanratty positively, and sympathy for her plight contributed to a feeling of hostility against the accused. He failed to establish a more reasonable account of his movements, and was executed.

Then Alphon made a number of 'confessions' to the crime, drawing attention to the fact that Gregsten was married, though living apart from his wife. Alphon said he had been approached in a pub by a friend of Mrs Gregsten's and hired to frighten Gregsten and Miss Storey into giving up their association.

Alphon made most of his public statements in France, beyond the jurisdiction of the English authorities. But Hanratty's admirable and respectable family, who had made heroic if unavailing efforts to pull him away from a life of crime, were anxious to have the case re-opened and James cleared of the charge of rape and murder.

The authorities were not keen to accord Hanratty a posthumous pardon, apparently feeling that there was enough circumstantial evidence to point to Hanratty as Gregsten's murderer. For on the night of the murder, Hanratty and Alphon were both registered under false names at the same hotel: The Hotel Vienna, 158–162 Sutherland Avenue. It is a very clean conversion of three tall brick terrace houses in a peaceful tree-lined street running between Harrow Road and Maida Vale. With a clientele of decent young students and tourists, it seems an unlikely setting for London crooks. But in 1961 it was briefly managed by a man named Nudds, known to some associates as 'The Squealer'. And a cartridge case fired from the weapon that murdered Michael Gregsten was found in the room where Hanratty had stayed. Half a mile to the north, in the rather anonymous Boundary Road, Hanratty had spent a part of the summer with his friend Charles 'Dixie' France, to whom he confided his secret hiding place in double-decker buses. There was some suggestion of connections stretching through antique dealers from Hanratty to Mrs Gregsten's associates. And

Alphon knew Hanratty and despised him as an incompetent criminal.

Carlton Vale, running from Maida Vale to Kilburn Lane, was the scene of a gangland killing in 1956. Tommy 'Scarface' Smithson went to a boarding house at no *88* (demolished, now, for road widening), apparently to demand money from its Maltese landlord. While Smithson waited in the company of a woman lodger for the landlord's return, a maroon car drew up and two more Maltese from Whitechapel came into the house. Exactly what happened thereafter has been recounted in different ways, depending on whether Philip Ellul and Nick Spampinato were on trial for their lives, or were collecting fees for sensational accounts of the killing. But Smithson was shot. Ellul was convicted and then reprieved. Spampinato when safe from the courts published and retracted a confession that was almost more of a sadistic boast.

Ten years later it was alleged that Smithson had been killed in gang warfare over the lucrative Soho vice rackets. Anyway, Smithson died bloodily at Maltese hands at a time when Maltese racketeers were moving to dominate territory the cockney East Enders had hoped to make theirs.

West of Paddington, Bayswater lies to the north of Hyde Park, an area of late-Victorian middle-class residential streets with a thriving shopping region centred on Queensway and Westbourne Grove. Today the old department stores are closing. Ethnic shops and restaurants are increasing, and some youthful night-life is flourishing in the wake of the seedy street-prostitution to which Stephen Ward and Christine Keeler went slumming in the 1960s.

William Whiteley was one of the first millionaire department-store founders. Whiteleys in Queensway has recently

closed and stands empty and magnificent. But when the
original Mr Whiteley was shot on his own premises, the
store stood in **Westbourne Grove** at 55–57. Horace
Rayner forced his way into the magnate's office demanding
an interview; shot him when he refused to listen, and
then turned his pistol on himself, mutilating his face and
destroying one eye.

His story elicited considerable sympathy. He believed
himself to be Whiteley's illegitimate son, and established
that the old man had enjoyed successive relationships with
his mother and her sister, who had been left inadequately
provided to give Rayner a good start in life. Since Whiteley
was a self-publicizing evangelical moralist his hypocrisy
and stinginess disgusted the public, and Rayner's reprieve
was very popular.

Alongside the Wesleyan Church at Inverness Place in
Queensway stands an imposing terrace of Victorian bourgeois residences. In 1858 this was called Rifle Terrace, and
Dr and Mrs Thomas Smethurst lodged at no 4. During
that year Miss Isabella Banks also took lodgings in the
house, and Dr Smethurst and she gave such obvious signs
of enjoying each other's intimate companionship that the
landlady asked Miss Banks to leave. She moved into new
lodgings at 37 Kildare Terrace, no distance away, off
Westbourne Grove, and the infatuated doctor abandoned
his wife and joined her. In December the two went through
a form of marriage at Battersea parish church, and moved
down to Richmond to lodge at 27 Old Palace Gardens, by
the green.

There Miss Banks was taken ill. In April the couple
moved to *120 Alma Villas*, **Richmond**, and Miss Banks
grew worse. Her sister Louise was summoned from 10
Langhart Villas, Maida Vale, to nurse her, but the lady
still declined. Smethurst called in two other doctors who

agreed that the lady was being poisoned. When she died, Smethurst was arrested, tried and convicted.

But the autopsy had failed to reveal any poison, and so Smethurst had been convicted on no evidence stronger than the opinion of two colleagues whom he had himself called in. He was reprieved, jailed for a year for bigamy, and freed. Immediately and successfully he applied for Miss Banks's estate which had been willed to him, and went to live at 137 Tachbrook Street, Pimlico.

Ginter Widra was representative of the more cosmopolitan and Bohemian population of Bayswater in the twentieth century. This 34-year-old Polish art student lived in the basement flat at **21 Leinster Square** in 1957. He was a paranoid depressive, and formed the delusion that his girlfriend Margaret Allen was seeing other men and posing for pornographic photographs. In a fit of jealousy he killed her with a samurai sword, and stabbed his landlady who tried to intervene. He was sent to Broadmoor.

Over the Serpentine and Long Water, Hyde Park becomes Kensington Gardens. Beyond Kensington Palace, at the western edge of the gardens, lie the socially mixed regions of West London. Patches of stucconia in Notting Hill mix with detached villas around Holland Park and Shepherd's Bush. These are inter-set with more densely populated streets of late nineteenth-century artisans' housing and modern council blocks. To the south, Kensington High Street runs through Hammersmith to the anonymous Chiswick High Road, and Cromwell Road becomes Talgarth Road and crosses Hammersmith Flyover to become the Great West Road. The two great arteries to London airport and the west country show little sign of the old villages which once surrounded them, and have been built over as populous but rather characterless suburbs, lightened by occasional small greens and commons.

Bayswater Road runs westward into the broad street of shops that is Notting Hill Gate. To the north Notting Hill lies along the spine of Ladbroke Grove. To the south Holland Park stretches down towards Kensington, flanked by quiet and dignified residential streets. Notting Hill has been richly endowed with twentieth-century murderers. Holland Park has not.

The most famous Notting Hill killer was the classic serial necrophile, John Reginald Halliday Christie. His infamous address, *10 Rillington Place*, was renamed *Ruston Close* soon after his execution. In the early 1970s the entire cul-de-sac of tiny three-floor terraced houses was pulled down, leaving only the quaint squared cone of factory chimney that had once lowered over a brick wall at the end of Christie's street. Today's Ruston Mews is still overlooked by the Metropolitan Line as it passes from Ladbroke Grove to Latimer Road, but is otherwise quite unreminiscent of the setting for seven women's deaths between 1943 and 1953.

'Reg' Christie, a Yorkshireman, served in the first World War, married Ethel Waddington in 1920, left her a few years later, and moved to London where he drifted into an unstable life of petty crime. In 1929 he was convicted of assaulting a woman with a cricket bat. But this was obviously rage rather than sexual taste. By the end of the 1930s he appeared to have settled down to life as a stock clerk, and his wife rejoined him. They moved into the tiny ground-floor flat in the end house at Rillington Place.

During the second war Christie concealed his criminal record and enrolled as a special policeman. The opportunity to exert petty authority appealed to the uptight surface of his repressed nature. The chance to visit sordid haunts of low-class prostitutes delighted its seamy underside.

During these years he discovered the excitement of killing a woman and copulating with her corpse. On two occasions while Mrs Christie was away visiting family he inveigled women acquaintances back to the flat and lulled them into inhaling Friars Balsam from a rigged jar into which he was also releasing gas. When they were asphyxiated he strangled them and abused their lifeless bodies. Ruth Fuerst and Murial Eady were buried under cover of darkness in the little garden at the back of the house. When Ruth Fuerst's skull rose to the surface, Christie took it away and threw it into the bombed house at 133 St Mark's Road, beside the tennis court in Kensington Memorial Park. When it was found, it was assumed to belong to a blitz victim. Her thighbone also surfaced and Christie used it to prop up a weak spot in the garden fence.

After the war, a little Welsh van driver called Timothy John Evans moved into the top-floor flat with his wife Beryl and their baby Geraldine. Irresponsibility, limited intelligence and habitual lying unsuited Evans for the role of paterfamilias. The family budget could scarcely afford his habitual evenings at his local, the Kensington Park Hotel in Ladbroke Grove. He and Beryl quarrelled about money, and occasionally he knocked her about. They quarrelled when she found herself pregnant again in 1949. Beryl knew they could not afford the second child and wanted an abortion. Evans disapproved.

In November he suddenly turned up on relatives in Wales with money in his pockets and time on his hands. He offered no adequate explanation, and impulsively destroyed any hope of subsequent police or Home Office sympathy by voluntarily going to the local police station and making an unprompted false confession to having thrown Beryl's body down the manhole outside 10 Rillington Place.

The Welsh police telephoned London. The Metropolitan police found the manhole, but established that it took four men to raise the cast-iron cover, and there was definitely no body at the bottom. But Beryl Evans and Geraldine were not in the flat, and Evans's furniture had gone.

With his lies exposed, Evans made a second statement. In this he claimed that Beryl had died following an unsuccessful abortion performed by Christie, who had disposed of the body; that Evans had sold his furniture to Mr Hookway of 319 Portobello Road; that Geraldine was being looked after by a couple in East Acton; and that to the best of his knowledge Christie had placed the body in the manhole. Since Ludovic Kennedy's investigation of the case in *10 Rillington Place* most people have assumed that Evans believed this statement to be entirely true, and that in fact Christie had used the promise of abortion to gain access to Beryl undressed and alone; that he killed her in his usual way, and told Evans the abortion had failed. Further, it is assumed that, after helping Evans carry the body downstairs, he told the bereaved husband that he had 'disposed of it' down the manhole, and arranged for a young couple in East Acton to look after Geraldine.

Evans was brought to London for further questioning at Ladbroke Grove. By the time he arrived, the police had found the strangled bodies of Beryl and Geraldine hidden in a tiny wash-house at the back of Rillington Place.

At this point nobody doubted that Evans had committed the murders. He had given himself up spontaneously. He had been known to quarrel violently with Beryl and beat her up. It looked like a typical domestic murder under the pressures of tight budgeting and living in a confined space. Evans's compulsive lying made it easy to disregard his involvement of Christie. And no one saw any reason to doubt Evans's third statement, which was a full and plausible confession to both murders.

Although he retracted this at his trial and reverted to accusing Christie, he could not even convince his own counsel. For the next five years his immediate family and the priest who attended his last days were the only people with any doubts about the justice of the obscure Evans's execution.

At Christmas 1953 intimates of Ethel Christie who normally heard from her at the festive season received a jolly little note from Reg explaining that his wife had hurt her hand so he was writing on her behalf, and adding that he would be cooking the Christmas dinner. It was completely untrue. For reasons still unknown, Christie had killed his wife and buried her under his sitting-room floorboards. He sprinkled the floor daily with disinfectant to mask the smell and drifted into an increasingly hopeless pattern of life. He went back to the small cafés and the unprotected prostitutes. Within two weeks in February he lured three separately back to his home, sat them down in a dirty string-mesh deck chair, strangled them, abused their bodies, and dumped them in a small alcove off the kitchen.

No disinfectant could stop his home from stinking now. He papered over the alcove and made quick, illegal arrangements to move out. He sold his furniture to Mr Hookway, and found a young couple to whom he offered to sublet. With their advance rent he wandered away and disappeared into the London crowds.

The neighbourhood was changing. West Indians were moving in, to the disgust of the rigid and perverted Christie. The house had been sold to a Jamaican. And the new landlord was shocked by the state of Christie's flat and by his illegal subtenants. In no time he had relet it to a compatriot who could be expected to clean it up. On his first day, the new tenant discovered that a part of the kitchen wall was mere paper. And that there was a woman's body behind the paper . . .

Christie's name was burned into the public mind while

the police hunted him and meanwhile discovered more and more bodies in his little mausoleum: Kathleen Maloney, Rita Nelson and Hectorina MacLennon in the alcove; Ethel under the floorboards; Ruth Fuerst and Muriel Eady in the garden. The bald dome and flashing spectacles of John Reginald Halliday Christie whom the police wished to interview in connection with the Notting Hill murders stared out of all the daily papers until an alert policeman recognized the face gazing moodily into the Thames at Putney Bridge.

At his trial he pleaded insanity, and confessed to seven murders including that of Beryl Evans. Since he remarked at one point, 'The more the merrier!' some cynics doubted his confession. (He never confessed to little Geraldine's murder.) But common sense revolted at the notion that one tiny house containing a very active, perverse murderer also happened to contain an ordinary domestic murderer who quite coincidentally (and with no knowledge of his proclivities) selected the necrophile from all possible neighbours to accuse falsely of a crime he had committed himself.

Still the police and the Home Office stoutly maintained that an incredible coincidence was indeed the case. They pointed to Evans's confession and to the frequency of husband/wife murders as compared to the rarity of necrophile murders. But in the end it was obvious that the course of Evans's interrogation and trial would have been enormously different had it been known that Christie had already compulsively killed two women. With a rather bad grace the authorities finally permitted the Welshman's re-burial and granted a posthumous free pardon. His was the most dramatic of the suspect executions leading to the eventual abolition of capital punishment for murder.

Notting Hill's next best known murderer was driven, like Christie, by sexual compulsion but operated in less squalid surroundings. **Pembridge Gardens** is a road of large stucco houses lined with flowering trees. **Pembridge Court** is one of many converted to private hotels. Here in 1946 Neville George Clevely Heath, a good-looking young officer and gentleman whose petty dishonesty and claim to names and ranks he did not possess had blemished his war and post-war career, took room 4 for a night. Here he brought Mrs Margery Gardner, a 32-year-old film extra whom he had met in the Panama Club, Knightsbridge. They were attracted by complementary sexual tastes: Mrs Gardner was a masochist and looked forward to being bound and beaten by Heath. She did not anticipate being beaten so severely that the woven mesh of the riding-whip he used would imprint its pattern in vivid bruises on her back and breasts. She did not expect him to bite her nipple so hard that he almost tore it off. She had not bargained for having a poker forced into her vagina so savagely that she died of her injuries.

Heath left her body there and went down to Bournemouth. He adopted the alias of 'Group-Captain Rupert Brooke', and registered at the Tollard Royal Hotel where 21-year-old Doreen Marshall met him. She was recuperating from measles and was captivated by Heath's charm and good looks. He beat and killed her after going for an evening walk, and his attempt to establish an abili by climbing into his hotel room via scaffolding and a builder's ladder failed. Nor could he conceal that his identity was that of the guest in the Pembridge Court for whom the police were searching.

Pembridge Gardens lead into the southwest corner of Pembridge Square. At the opposite corner is **Chepstow Place**, where the body of a black marketeer known as 'Russian Robert' was found in a small car in 1945. Reuben Martirosoff's known associates were traced, and a couple of deserters from the Polish Freedom Fighters, Marian Grondowski and Henry Malinowski were unable to give a good account of themselves. In the end they accused each other of shooting Martirosoff and were both hanged. They had quarrelled with him over black marketeering. The police were happy to close the file on Frank 'The Duke' Everitt, whose body had been found shot in the Fire Service pumping house that then stood on **Lambeth Bridge**, while his taxi had been abandoned not far from Chepstow Place. 'The Duke', too, had dabbled in the black market.

Clarendon Road, by Holland Park tube station, largely comprises decent terraced houses. But **no 13** near the Holland Park Avenue end is one gracious half of a large, square, semi-detached stucco box separated by gardens from the pavement. In 1919 Sir Malcolm Seton owned it and his cousin Miles was staying there. The occupants were gentlemanly and unflappable when neighbours who had been disturbed by the sound of shots came round to investigate. They dismissed all offers of help, did their own tidying up and decorously informed the police that a murder had taken place.

Miles was shot by his friend Dr Norman Rutherford, whose wife had decided to leave him. Shell-shock had rendered Rutherford unstable and unpredictable, and while this sufficiently explained Mrs Rutherford's estrangement it also left him resentful of friends from whom she had taken advice. He assumed that Miles was her lover; regretted his mistake before his victim died; and was committed to Broadmoor.

The Mitre was until very recently a neat modern pub on the corner of Ladbroke Grove and Holland Park Avenue. Now it is a wine bar. On a January morning in 1974, Terence Noonan and Edward Wilkinson waited there for a summons to the writer James Pope-Hennessy's home at **9 Ladbroke Grove**. Not that the young men knew Pope-Hennessy, author of the official life of Queen Mary. But their friend Sean O'Brien had met and stayed with him. It was reported that the writer had been paid an advance of £150,000 for a life of Noel Coward. And the three had decided to make that money their own.

James Pope-Hennessy was a homosexual, living contentedly with his valet-companion Leslie Walker-Smith. O'Brien had been picked up by Pope-Hennessy and Walker-Smith and spent a few nights with them the previous month. He had learned his way around their house, and now proposed to use his friends to rob his patrons. He waited until Walker-Smith went out in the late morning (to buy a carving knife) and called Noonan and Wilkinson over.

The three young thugs attacked Pope-Hennessy, tied him up, and demanded the £150,000. Since he had not yet received it, their expectation of marching out cash in hand was sadly misplaced. And the plan went further astray when Walker-Smith returned, armed with the new carving knife.

In the resulting fracas, Walker-Smith was injured. Pope-Hennessy was killed, and the three young men escaped, not entirely unscathed. They were identified, traced and arrested within a couple of days, and the case against them was so clear-cut that they ultimately pled 'Guilty' at their trial.

South of Holland Park Avenue there has been significantly less murder. Jack the Stripper (p. 143) dumped his penultimate victim in **Hornton Street**, which runs into High Street Kensington. A nasty unsolved child murder took place in 1931 when 11-year-old Vera Page was found raped and strangled in the tradesman's entrance of *89* **Addison**

Road. (This also runs into Kensington High Street but at
the Holland Road end rather than the Kensington Church
Street end. The house no longer stands, but was similar to
the other villas set a little back in this road.) She had last
been seen in Notting Hill turning into Lansdowne Crescent
from Lansdowne Rise. A great deal of circumstantial
evidence led to charges being brought against a man in
whose area cellar it seemed that her body might have been
kept briefly. But the grand jury failed to find a true bill
against him, and he was released. This happened while
George Cornish was the reigning 'Knacker of the Yard' – a
prominent detective whose charged suspects went uncon-
victed so often that one supposes he was unusually scrupu-
lous in his interrogations, investigations and presentation
of evidence.

Harold Dorien Trevor was a persistent and incompetent
criminal, ending his career as an easily detected murderer.
He was nearly sixty in 1941 and had spent most of the
previous forty years in prison for a succession of unsuccessful frauds. In his last brief stretch of freedom he saw a flat
advertised to let in **Elsham Road**. This long yellow-brick
terrace parallel to Holland Road is made attractive by the
many trees in the front gardens and the stucco ornamen-
tation of doors and windows. The large houses are still for
the most part divided into flats.

Trevor did not actually want to live in the basement flat
at **71a**. His hope was to gain admittance as a prospective
tenant, case the joint, and rob the comfortable middle-
class accommodation.

Elderly Mrs Theodora Greenhill was delighted when a
well-spoken man who claimed to be a doctor (Trevor was
an experienced confidence trickster) came to look round.
He inspected the premises, agreed to take them and prepared to pay a deposit before he terminated the visit by

strangling the old lady. He left the flat full of his well-known fingerprints, and an unfinished receipt in the old lady's hand made out to 'Dr H. D. Trevor'. One feels that police pleasure in the recidivist's continued incompetence was tempered by regret that this uncharacteristically violent crime inevitably led him to the scaffold.

West London, from Brentford to Kensington, was extensively traversed by the Acton-based motorized multiple murderer of the 1960s, 'Jack the Stripper'. Although never charged or publicly named, this killer was identified by painstaking police work and committed suicide when he realized that his arrest was imminent.

The 'Nudes-in-the-Thames' murders, as they were known in 1964, drew attention to a stretch of the Boat Race course from Barnes Bridge to **Hammersmith Bridge**. The naked body of prostitute Hannah Tailford was washed up beside the latter on February 2nd. Two months later Irene Lockwood's body drifted on to **Duke's Meadow**, the large sports and recreation ground dominating the Chiswick bank of the narrow bend in the river three hundred yards upstream.

The previous year, two other murdered prostitutes had been found hereabouts at the riverside: Elizabeth Figg in June and Gwynneth Rees in November. The police realized that they were hunting for a maniac.

As the river bank grew more heavily patrolled, 'Jack the Stripper', as he was soon nicknamed, began dumping his bodies inland. On April 24th Helene Barthelemy was found in a lane between the first and second garages in **Swyncombe Avenue, Brentford**, leading to the sports ground. In July Mary Fleming's body was left in a garage entrance in **Berymede Road, off Acton Lane**. (This site was the first to be remote from any playing field or recreation ground.) It seemed likely that the killer had been driving a small van which was reported for dangerous driving as it reversed alarmingly out of the small residential cul-de-sac on to Acton Lane. Unfortunately the report did not carry its number or an identifiable description.

But the bodies themselves were cumulatively yielding fresh evidence. Semen traces and missing teeth revealed that the girls had choked to death while they performed fellatio on the murderer. It seemed, too, that he kept their bodies and possibly abused them after death.

Paint specks indicated that the bodies had been held near a workshop using a paint-sprayer on car bodies. And obviously the stripper drove a van in the vicinity of Chiswick, Brentford and Acton, and was familiar with the sports grounds of the area.

Habitual night-drivers in West London were stopped and required to account for themselves. This steady pressure produced four murder-free months, and then a rather surprising change of dumping place. In November, Margaret McGowan was carried back toward the West End and dropped in the car park outside the municipal offices in **Hornton Street, off Kensington High Street**. (The municipal buildings have now been extended across the site.) This was very different from the unpretentious lower-middle-class suburbia where the previous bodies had rested.

The end came three months later. A heavy blanket of police coverage convinced detectives that their man had been in their hands on several occasions, talking his way to freedom because his employment justified his driving around West London at night. They had narrowed their attention to three definite suspects. By February police patrols made it unsafe for the murderer to carry his final victim far afield for deposit: Bridie O'Hara's body was found at the **Westpoint Trading Estate in West Acton** where, at last, the spray-shop and adjacent warehouse where the bodies had been kept were located. At the same time, a security guard working on the estate, one of the three police suspects, committed suicide, leaving an ambiguous note to the effect that the pressure was too much for him. There were no further murders, and the police were satisfied that the file could be closed.

In 1944 Elizabeth Jones was working as an exotic dancer in the Blue Lagoon Club, Carnaby Street (where Margaret Cook (p. 62) was found dead two years later), and the Panama Club, Knightsbridge (where Neville Heath (p. 138) met Margery Gardner). 'Marina', as the Welsh stripper was professionally known, had digs at 311 King Street, Hammersmith. And in a nearby café on the corner of Hammersmith Broadway and Queen Caroline Street (now covered by the Hammersmith flyover) she met a young GI named Karl Hulten. He passed himself off as a lieutenant and called himself 'Ricky', and he impressed her by pretending to be a Chicago gangster.

Hulten's showing-off led quickly to crime. He commandeered his army jeep and went AWOL with Elizabeth Jones. They waylaid two girl cyclists and stole a handbag from one. A day later they hailed George Heath's taxi on the Hammersmith Road adjacent to Cadby Hall (next to Olympia) and got him to drive them to the **Great West Road**. There Hulten shot him, probably to impress Jones as much as anything.

They were a pair of silly amateurs, playing at tough guys in imitation of the movies. Though most of their territory has been subjected to intensive road-widening, the Hammersmith Road still presents some of the drab anonymity to which they tried to bring their own form of spurious glamour. Since Hulten was a serving US soldier it was a matter of some constitutional and diplomatic importance that the American authorities let him be tried

by a British court and executed by a British hangman.
Jones was reprieved.

The search for glamour continued forty years later. Hammersmith Hospital was embarrassed in 1982 when it was shown that misdiagnosis or the mishandling of records had caused an eleven-month delay before they established that the death of a patient had been caused by paraquat poisoning.

Michael Barber had been displeased to arrive home and find his wife Susan in bed with the couple's friend, Richard Collier. He reacted by throwing Collier out and beating Susan. A week later he was dead. Half a teaspoonful of weedkiller in his dinner induced an illness which brought him to hospital and death. Susan happily set up home with Collier, but found that relationship, too, unsatisfactory. By the time she was apprehended she had been advertising for a new lover on Citizens' Band Radio under the name of 'Nympho'. She was arrested and convicted of murder; and Collier was convicted of conspiracy to murder.

Cardross Street, Hammersmith (four blocks east of Ravenscourt Park), was known as 'Rose Garden' in 1865 when Kate Webster took lodgings there in no 16 Brightwell Cottages. She became friendly with a family named Porter living next door, and told them that she was going into domestic service in Norland Crescent (presumably Royal Crescent, abutting Norland Square), Notting Hill. In fact she had a baby. Then she served an eighteen-month prison sentence for fraud and theft.

In 1876 she moved down to Richmond, Surrey, working for Mrs Julia Thomas at *2 Vine Cottages* (soon renamed **Mayfield**) in **Park Road**, parallel to Richmond Hill between Friar's Stile Road and Queen's Road.

In March 1879 Kate paid a visit to her old friends the

Porters in Hammersmith. They had not seen her for six years, and were surprised to notice her expensive clothes, good jewellery and watch. She told them she had been married and widowed since she last saw them and was now Mrs Thomas. She said she wanted to sell her house and furniture. She persuaded them to let young Bobby Porter see her home, to help her with a heavy bag she was carrying. On the way she left Bobby for a moment and went on to Hammersmith Bridge. When she returned the bag was no longer with her.

Back at Mayfield she got Bobby to help her carry a large heavy box out of the house, along Mt Ararat Road, and down Paradise Road to Richmond Bridge. After this half-mile journey they rested the box on the nearer of the two recesses at the centre of the bridge, and Kate sent Bobby back to the Surrey bank, saying she had to meet someone on the Middlesex side. Bobby heard a loud splash, and Kate reappeared without the box.

The next day, a large box was recovered from the Thames alongside The Terrace at Barnes Bridge. It contained several boiled parts of a woman.

Kate, meanwhile, had been introduced by the Porters to John Church, who kept a beershop called The Rising Sun in Rose Garden. He was interested in buying 'Mrs Thomas's' furniture and getting to know her more intimately. He spent two or three nights alone with her at Mayfield. But he was serious about the furniture, and hired a van to load it up and remove it. Porter came along to help him.

While they worked a neighbour came out and demanded to know whether Mrs Thomas was aware that they were removing her things. The men confidently assured her that she knew, and called Kate out to prove it. It became apparent that Kate was *not* Mrs Thomas in her neighbour's eyes, and didn't pretend to be. Both men realized that 'something wasn't right'.

Kate fled. She raced back to Hammersmith, borrowed a guinea from Church's wife, and made all haste by rail and sea to Ireland.

It was of no avail. The house was examined by the police. A thorough cleaning job had been done in the kitchen, but there was still a suspicious fatty scum in the copper. Kate had washed a lot of clothes at an unusual hour on the last day Mrs Thomas had been seen alive. It was recalled that Mrs Thomas had given Kate notice the day she disappeared. It was pretty clear that the bag she had taken to tea at the Porters had contained Mrs Thomas's head, and the box she and Bobby had lugged to the Thames had contained what was left of Mrs Thomas after she had been dismembered and boiled in the copper. It was whispered that Kate had gone around Richmond offering jars of fresh dripping for sale the following day . . .

Kate Webster was one of the worst, as she was one of the last, notorious servant-murderers.

Acton is attractive lower-middle-class suburbia, with well-tended gardens and quiet greens setting off well-painted and maintained semi-detached houses. This is true of the little complex of streets around East Acton station leading to the large common of Wormwood Scrubs, with the massive prison overlooking its southern corner.

Braybrook Street is often misleadingly described as being in Shepherd's Bush. It is on the edge of Wormwood Scrubs, with houses on the inner side only, so that their view across the road and common is undisturbed. At the western end the prison is out of sight. The rising grassy bank opposite is known as Old Oak Common, and beyond it tall house backs arise beyond hidden railway lines. It is a light, open peaceful road: an unlikely site for the brutal killing of three policemen.

John Witney, John Duddy and Harry Roberts were small-time north London criminals. Witney lived in a basement flat in Fernhead Road, Paddington; Duddy in Treverton Towers, Ladbroke Grove, Roberts, in August 1966, was staying with Mrs Marion Perry in Wymering Mansions, Wymering Road, Maida Vale. On a fine summer morning the three gathered at the Clay Pigeon in Field End Road, Ruislip, and planned to steal a car for a robbery. They drove in Witney's car back to Braybrook Street, where they paused to plan their next move. Police 'Q' car Foxtrot 11 was on duty there. Detective Sergeant Christopher Head, Detective Constable David Wombwell and PC David Fox wondered what a lonely car with three men in it was doing, parked with no apparent good purpose around the bend from Wormwood Scrubs prison. It was a matter of routine to go over and investigate.

The three crooks foresaw their arrest on trivial charges before they had started on the day's work. Even so, Witney and Duddy were astonished when Roberts' response to the first policeman's firm questions was to pull a gun and shoot him dead. There followed four minutes of mayhem as the other two policemen alternately tried to go to their fallen comrade's assistance, to take cover, and to drive away. It ended with all three policemen pointlessly dead in Braybrook Street, and the shocked crooks driving helter-skelter for a lock-up garage under a railway arch near Waterloo where they dumped the car and split up.

Though it was Roberts whose spontaneous violence had unleashed the manhunt, all three were collectively guilty of murder, since they had intended to break the law and resist arrest. Duddy fled to Glasgow. Roberts moved into the Russell Hotel with Mrs Perry. Witney went home, where the police soon traced him after they had found the van and were unconvinced by his impromptu story of having sold it earlier that day to an unknown man in a pub.

Duddy was soon picked up in Scotland. But Roberts went with Mrs Perry to East London where he bought camping equipment, took leave of her at the Wakefield Arms, Park Road E10, tearfully recognizing that he had 'made a mess of things', and set off in the direction of Epping Forest to live rough.

For three months his whereabouts was unknown. Then a schoolboy spotted his secret camp miles away from Epping Forest in Thorley Wood near Bishop's Stortford in Hertfordshire. Roberts was arrested without incident. And so ended one of the most shocking killings of policemen going quietly about their duty.

Turnham Green was once a village, famous in the annals of murder for *Linden House*, which stood in four acres of its own grounds on **Chiswick High Road** (where **Linden Gardens** today almost face the Windmill complex). In the 1820s this house was owned by elderly George Griffiths, whose heir was the young journalist, engraver and fop, Thomas Griffiths Wainewright. The nephew preferred living close to Regent Street, and fell heavily in debt while lodging at 49 Great Marlborough Street. To mend his fortunes he went to stay with his uncle, and hastened his inheritance by poisoning the old man.

But becoming master of Linden House in 1829 did not relieve Wainewright of all financial embarrassment, so he insured the life of his sister-in-law, Helen Abercrombie, hoping to dispose of her conveniently. Helen's mother, however, had to be poisoned first. By the time Wainewright got round to poisoning Helen, he was able to dismiss the sordid thought of money from his dandy's mind. 'Her ankles were so thick' was his insouciant explanation when later taxed with murder.

He returned to town in 1830, taking up residence at 12 Conduit Street. But now the insurance companies caught up with him. He was arrested, not for murder, but forgery (an equally capital charge). He was lucky to be sentenced to transportation.

While he awaited shipment to Australia 'Janus Weathercock' (his journalistic *nom-de-plume*) made his first footnote in the annals of great literature. Charles Dickens was slumming with a small group of friends, when, in the depths of Newgate Prison, the actor Macready cried out, 'My God, it's Wainewright!' The literary party were disconcerted to find a social acquaintance among the human derelicts.

Wainewright's second claim to fame was as the subject of Oscar Wilde's essay *Pen, Pencil and Poison*. A kind and unwittingly moral man, Wilde was obviously perturbed by the potential heartlessness and immorality of his own theory of 'art for art's sake', and wrote fiction eschewing it. This essay gives it an ironical *reductio ad absurdum*.

By association, Wainewright leads us westward to Ealing. Little Ealing Lane runs from Northfield Avenue and Windmill Road, New Brentford (near Jack the Stripper's Swyncombe Avenue (p. 143)) to South Ealing Road and Pope's Lane. Here, in 1828, Wainewright found Grove House, a suitable establishment for a pair of newlywed friends who wanted to open a private school.

Young William Corder had only recently come to London. While staying at the Bull Inn, Leadenhall Street, he had met the young woman he swiftly married and established as a schoolmistress with Wainewright's blessing.

Their domestic bliss was short-lived. Corder's friends

and relatives in Polstead, Suffolk, believed that he was already married to a village girl. But a peculiar suspicion, later explained as the outcome of a dream, led Maria Marten's mother to have the 'old red barn' searched, and her daughter's body was found buried there. The murder became famous in Victorian melodrama wherein Maria was portrayed as the innocent victim of a cruel seducer. Actually she was a casually promiscuous young woman who already had two illegitimate children when she entrapped Corder into a promise of marriage. He murdered her, buried the body in the barn, and pretended that they had both gone away for a honeymoon. Corder, who brought great notoriety to his home village, was arrested in Ealing.

A hundred years later Ealing was a large, comfortable borough. Linford Derrick, a tennis coach, was friendly with Mr and Mrs Arthur Wheeler of **Winscombe Crescent** (in the maze of residential streets south of Western Avenue, not far from the Ealing and Hanger Hill golf courses). But jealousy intruded on the friendship in 1936. Mr Wheeler accused Mr Derrick of conducting a liaison with Mrs Wheeler, and attacked him with a truncheon. In the ensuing fight, Mr Derrick had the misfortune to prove that a quick, clean blow over the head with a blunt instrument does not result in the brief and harmless concussion suggested by the movies. He killed Mr Wheeler and then, panicking, disordered the house to suggest a robbery. Happily he recovered his senses before he had committed himself to the lie, and gave himself up to the police. In consequence his crime was accepted as manslaughter, and he was not hanged.

Three roads south of Winscombe Crescent, the slightly more spacious **Montpelier Avenue** runs from east to west. Two ladies ran an old people's home at no 22 in the 1950s. Vera Chesney and her mother, who assumed the title of

Lady Menzies, supported themselves in the absence abroad of Vera's husband Ronald.

A buccaneering figure with a beard and a gold earring, Ronald Chesney had enjoyed a 'good war', ending up with a prosperous hand in the West German black market. But the piping times of peace were less fruitful for this hearty rogue, and by 1954 he was keen to convert the wife he did not support into a corpse whose assets he could inherit. To this end he shaved off his beard, acquired a false passport and travelled to England hoping the false identity would leave him with a secure alibi and his alcoholic wife's death would be passed off as a drunken fall in the bath.

He had reckoned without Lady Menzies. The need to batter her to death when she recognized him revealed that two murders had been committed by an intruder who new the house intimately, and his escape to the continent did not mean escape from Interpol. The police tracked him to a wood in West Germany where he shot himself.

Then it was realized that black marketeer and confidence trickster Ronald Chesney was none other than John Donald Merrett, notorious in Scotland in the 1920s as a young man who had escaped with a 'Not Proven' verdict after being tried for matricide. As a 'student', Merrett had systematically forged his mother's signature on cheques. When she found her bank account overdrawn he happened to be in the room with her. She was found shot through the head a few minutes later, and the jury agreed that it was possible that she had shot herself, as Merrett claimed.

9

—————— Northwest London ——————

Highgate Hill runs northwest from Archway tube station, parallel with Archway Road. To the east lies a brick-terraced London that Mr Pooter would have recognized: essentially it is north Holloway. To the west leafier hilly roads and vast blocks of semi-private mansion flats lead to Hampstead Heath, the most unspoiled open space preserved from the countryside that surrounded a smaller London. At the southwestern corner of the Heath, Hampstead Village struggles to retain a community identity characterized by vague recollections of Keats hearing nightingales and a large upper-middle-class presence ensuring plentiful 'good-taste' shops.

Back at the Holloway end of the region in 1914 a monster of bad taste calling himself 'Mr Lloyd' was looking for lodgings in *Bismarck Road*. (*That* name didn't survive the war to end wars, and is today **Waterlow Road**, between Highgate Hill and Archway Road). In this typical terrace of cramped, two-storey brick houses with rather topheavy Corinthian capitalled pillars at the doors and windows, Mr Lloyd rented the upper floor of **no 14**. With him he brought his newlywed wife.

Mr Lloyd was most solicitous of his good lady's health and insisted that she see Dr Bates of 30 Archway Road. She seemed healthy to the doctor, but he accepted the story of her unaccountable dizzy spells and headaches.

On December 15th Mr Lloyd played a few bars of

'Nearer, my God, to Thee' on the harmonium in his room and went out to buy tomatoes for supper. On his return he went to see whether Mrs Lloyd had finished the bath she had been taking when he left. To his apparent horror, she had passed out and drowned. He called the landlady and sent for Dr Bates who sadly agreed that another dizzy spell must have overtaken her, causing her to lose consciousness as she slipped under water. Mr Lloyd rapidly arranged for her funeral.

But press reports of the unusual death in London attracted the attention of two families in Herne Bay and Southsea. They, too, had lost recently married relatives who drowned in their baths. They, too, had known a bereaved widower who used medical examinations to establish suppositious 'fits' before the tragedy, and absconded fast afterwards. One father-in-law had mistrusted the fellow and opposed the marriage. One landlady had called the sorrowing widower 'Crippen' and predicted that he would be heard of again.

As he was. George Joseph Smith, the 'Brides-in-the-Bath' murderer, had devised an ingenious mode of domestic assassination which easily passed immediate question. But it could not survive repetition and publicity: it was too much of a coincidence that one man should suffer three extraordinary and identical bereavements in the space of four years. Nor did it help that Mr Smith was a professional swindler and bigamist. He offered lonely women marriage, and ruthlessly deserted them once he had gained control of their property or savings.

Beatrice Mundy at Herne Bay in 1910 and Alice Burnham at Southsea in 1912 were the first two he drowned. Although he realized substantial sums from these murders, Smith was, like many criminals, extravagant and feckless. And so Margaret Lofty became the third 'bride-in-the-bath', and Smith's criminal career ended, as it had begun, in London. (He was born at 92 Roman Road, Bethnal Green, and imprisoned for theft in his youth.)

It was easy for the prosecution to prove a pattern in Smith's bereavements. They even proved, by experiment on a nurse in a bathing suit, that it was quite difficult *not* to drown someone whose legs were pulled upward sharply while she lay in a bath. The nurse survived, but it was a nastier moment than anyone had anticipated.

Smith coarsely asserted his innocence and abused the court. Surprising numbers of women came to ogle the 'monster', who was convicted and hanged.

Millfield Lane runs along part of the eastern edge of Hampstead Heath, beside Highgate Ponds. It once led to a farm, and at the bottom of the lane, old farm cottages form **'Millfield Cottage'**, a most attractive listed building with some gentrified lead in the windows and a high black fence concealing it from the pond on whose bank it stands.

In 1814 a turncock named Dobbins lived here with his common-law wife Elizabeth Buchanan. While Dobbins was out at work, a passing vagrant named Thomas Sharpe gained admission to the kitchen and beat Elizabeth to death with the poker. Neighbours who saw the blood on the floor summoned Dobbins, and then waylaid Sharpe whose furtive retreat toward Highgate Hill aroused suspicion. He had stolen the Dobbinses' washing.

When Lord Ellenborough concluded his death sentence with the words 'and may the Lord have mercy on your soul', Sharpe solemnly responded, 'May the curse of God attend you day and night, both in this world and the next.'

Parliament Hill stands southwest of the ponds. One footpath over the hill runs directly into the street of comfortable houses itself called Parliament Hill, leading down to Hampstead Heath station. Parallel to this str   the west lies the similar **South Hill Park**, but this offers no direct access to the Heath as it curves back on itself at the top, renaming itself Hill Park Gardens as it does so. The last two women to be hanged in England both committed their murders in South Hill Park.

Many of the tall terraced houses have been divided into flats, and Stavros Christofi and his family lived on the ground floor of **no 11** in 1954. Stavros, a waiter, had lived in England for twelve years. His wife Hella was German, and they had two children. Their life was happy until his mother came over from Cyprus to join them. Mrs Styllou Christofi was the frightful mother-in-law to end all frightful mothers-in-law.

She was jealous, possessive and violent. In her youth this might have passed as the fiery mediterranean temperament of a passionate young woman. Certainly she had tolerated no opposition from her own mother-in-law: at the age of twenty-five she was acquitted of the charge of murdering her by forcing a flaming torch down her throat.

But a young woman with an uncontrollable romantic temperament may grow into an unlovable harridan. Mrs Christofi makes such a description seem generous.

She quarrelled with Hella. She criticized the children's upbringing. She disliked England and could not master English. Ultimately the tantrums and drama were too much for Hella who arranged to take the children on holiday to Germany and insisted that her mother-in-law must be back in Cyprus before her return.

Mrs Christofi had no intention of being sent home at her daughter-in-law's behest, though she agreed that one of them must leave. She made sure it was Hella by battering her with the ashplate from the kitchen stove, strangling her as she lay on the kitchen floor, and setting fire to her. As a fire in the kitchen seemed inconvenient, she dragged the body out to the area behind the house (invisible from the street) where a neighbour reading at an upstairs window noticed her dumpy figure pass in and out, tending the flames. The fire had a somewhat human shape, and the neighbour assumed that Mrs Christofi was burning a tailor's dummy.

Eventually the old lady ran out into the street and persuaded a passer-by that there was a fire in her kitchen endangering the sleeping children. Her attempt to pass the incident off as an accident showed her to be as stupid as she was malevolent. The story of her former acquittal in Cyprus sealed her fate. From the condemned cell she grumbled that Stravros had neither visited nor saved her. She died remorseless, morally incapable of adult responsibility or regret.

Ruth Ellis was very different. While every bit as much a woman of feeling, she showed herself remarkably capable of accepting responsibility. Early pregnancy, early marriage and early divorce left her with two children and her own way to make in the world. She made it with the tawdry glamour of a nightclub hostess, and earned a little extra by putting out for favoured customers. But she was more than just a pretty face and an easy lay. She had a certain honesty and self-discipline which attracted the nightclub proprietor's attention, and soon she found herself employed as manageress of The Little Club at 37 Brompton Road, Knightsbridge, organizing the bar and till, controlling the staff, and comfortably earning her decent wage and free flat above the premises.

The raffish late-night drinking clientele included a core of motor-racing enthusiasts. From their ranks Ruth attracted the deep love of a steady, older bachelor businessman named Desmond Curren, and the roving eye of an unstable and drunken young driver named David Blakeley. He enjoyed sex with Ruth, and led her to hope they might become engaged, even though he was already nominally engaged to a 'suitable' girl from his family's circle. When they went to the motor races, his snobbish friends despised Ruth's lack of class, and she realized that his family could never accept her.

Worst of all, he made drunken scenes at the club until Ruth found herself out of her job and her flat. David was sulkily impenitent, and there seemed little she could do but accept Curren's offer of accommodation at his flat in Goodwood Court, Devonshire Street. But she was still hooked on her toy boy, and slept with David in Curren's bed and behind his back. When Blakeley complained about her living with Curren she moved out into a flat of her own at 44 Egerton Gardens.

Once she was freely available again, Blakeley typically lost interest. Friends of his in Hampstead disapproved of the liaison, and he yielded awkwardly to their pressure on him to give Ruth up. He went to stay with them at 29 Tanza Road (a steep side-road off Parliament Hill) and refused to accept Ruth's telephone calls. His surly and immature gracelessness outraged her. She persuaded Curren to drive her to Hampstead where, seeing David leave Tanza Road with his hosts' attractive young nanny, she jumped to the conclusion that this was a new lover who had displaced her. After a weekend of sullen brooding she borrowed a revolver from a still unidentified source, got herself over to Hampstead, and peered hopelessly through the contoured glass windows of **The Magdala Tavern** at the bottom of South Hill Park. David's car was parked outside, he having gone in to buy some beer for his hosts in Tanza Road.

When he emerged Ruth shot him. As he lay in the road she fired three more bullets into his body. Then she meekly gave herself up to a policeman in mufti who had been drinking in the pub, and did her best to secure conviction and execution as punishment for herself.

For Ruth Ellis was a simple moralist. She believed that having deliberately killed her lover it was right that she should be killed. Her counsel had the greatest difficulty in persuading her to plead 'Not Guilty', which in her eyes was a lie or a silly legal fiction. She rejected the efforts of the abolitionists who wanted her reprieved. With a pathetic attempt at dignity she addressed a mis-spelled letter to David's mother, accepting her own punishment, and obscurely hoping that Mrs Blakeley would somehow 'understand'.

Her death evoked vehement protest and was one of the three executions which did most to end capital punishment.

Northwest of Notting Hill the formal space of Queen's Park lies between the suburban areas of Kilburn and Kensal Rise. Some large cemeteries indicate that they were rather at the western edge of London in the early twentieth century.

Charteris Road is a drab street of terraced two-storey houses, a little difficult of access, in the vicinity of Paddington Cemetery. In the front bed-sittingroom of **no 58**, 31-year-old prostitute Veronica Murray was discovered, battered and mutilated in 1958. The murderer had left fingerprints, but as he had no criminal record these did not identify him. The same prints were found at a robbery in the Westbury Hotel, Westbury Avenue, Noel Park, early the following year.

They were next found in association with another violent sex crime. Mrs Mabel Hill had a flat at 5 Ismailia Road, which then linked Wandsworth Bridge Road with Townmead Road, just north of the bridge. In October 1959 a young man charmed his way into her flat where he tried to rape and strangle her. Mrs Hill survived to give a rough description of the owner of the now-familiar fingerprints.

They turned up again in a number of Chelsea burglaries. This time an unusual cigarette-lighter was among the stolen property, and its description was widely publicized. A comrade-in-arms shopped Michael Dowdall, a nineteen-year-old drummer in the Welsh Guards who had suddenly acquired just such a lighter, and the police had their murderer. He successfully pleaded diminished responsibility.

Wrentham Avenue, a long well-spaced street of uncluttered if rather dull two-storey terraces runs parallel with Chevening Road, just north west of Queen's Park. In 1903 it was called Ladysmith Avenue.

George Crossman rented part of his house in the avenue to William Dell. When Dell complained that there was an extremely nasty smell proceeding from the cupboard under the stairs, Crossman explained that a 'box of size' had 'gone bad', and made arrangements for carriers to come and remove it.

The box was a tin trunk. It was remarkably heavy and its stench was appalling. Crossman tried to mask it by lighting a cigar. But his nerve went completely when he saw a policeman outside in the avenue, and he amazed Mr Dell and the workmen by cutting his own throat.

Then it was learned that Crossman had accidentally carried out an experiment on the pressure exerted by gases released in decomposition. The 'box of size' was full of cement. The cement was full of Mrs Ellen Sampson, bigamist Crossman's fifth 'wife'. As her body decomposed and expanded it had cracked the cement and released the stinking gases which led to her removal and discovery. (Crossman had 'married' two more wives since packing Mrs Sampson tidily away under the stairs.)

Almost opposite the western end of Wrentham Avenue, Clifford Gardens proceeds westward. The houses here are more cramped, but the terraces are relieved by a wonderful builder's *jeu d'esprit*. Heavy swagged garlands in brick relief lie between the sitting-room and bedroom windows. The flat slab porches over the small front doors are converted by wrought-iron balustrades into tiny balconies. And the gables are fantastically enlivened by low cement reliefs: scrolled and curlicued shields and medallions; simple landscapes; vaguely neo-classical pastoral figures engaged in simple agricultural pursuits. It is sad to record that this Dickensian environment housed one of this century's most colourless murder victims.

Meagre, bespectacled undernourished Elsie Cameron met Norman Thorne at nearby Kensal Rise Wesleyan church. Young Thorne was not very successful after his demob in 1918, and in 1923 he left London to invest his small savings in a chicken farm at Crowborough, Sussex. In the meantime he and Elsie had become lovers and considered themselves engaged.

But in Sussex, Norman met a new and more exciting girl-friend. With hopeless determination Elsie packed her small weekend case, left 86 Clifford Gardens, and made for the railway to Sussex. With prim determination she was going to use the threat of her pregnancy to force Thorne into marriage.

She was not seen again after making her way to his small shed. Thorne claimed that she had never arrived. His aid to curious police and pressmen included allowing himself to be photographed on the very spot where he had buried her. When her body was discovered, he revived the old story, dating back to Daniel Good (p. 223), that he had found her a suicide, and fearing that suspicion would fall on him had panicked and hidden the body. There was no evidence to disprove his story, but it failed to convince the court, and he was hanged.

Willesden and Neasden, Cricklewood and Muswell Hill are full of early twentieth-century houses that could be anywhere in England. Their occupant murderers and victims, with a few exceptions, lack the flamboyance or squalor of more central killers, and professional crime has not carried on its gang wars here.

But from the west and east of this northern territorial sweep, two cases in 1896 showed true Victorian gusto.

Mrs Amelia Dyer, the baby farmer, looked the perfect turn-of-the-century little old lady with bright grey eyes, drab check shawl, and a hat like Old Mother Riley or Toad's washerwoman. Advertising herself as a foster-parent, she stressed her church-going. She used her married daughter Polly's house at **76 Mayo Road, Willesden** (off Church Road, a little way west of the cemetery) as a rendezvous to collect baby Doris Marmon from her mother. Mrs Dyer did not make sufficiently sure that Miss Marmon really wanted to see the last of her shameful bundle. Miss Marmon demanded to know where the baby had been taken from Willesden, and would not be fobbed off with evasions. In consequence, Arthur and Polly Palmer found themselves in dire danger of murder charges when clothing belonging to baby Doris and another baby, Harry Simmons, was found in their house, while the babies themselves were discovered, strangled, in the Thames at Reading.

Mrs Dyer disposed of her victims in Berkshire. The Marmon and Simmons babies were dropped in the water in a large carpet bag that she had been carrying at Willesden, and had presumably been killed there. But Mrs Dyer was most anxious to exonerate Polly and Arthur, and expressed profound Christian remorse for her sins. (So in the eyes of the law she knew she was doing wrong.)

Revulsion at her crimes and distaste for her glib sanctimoniousness obliterated the excellence of her defence. She
had been in and out of asylums regularly since 1891, and a
legal code more humane than the McNaghten Rules would
have sent her back there for good.

Away eastward in **Muswell Hill**, Mr Henry Smith's
fine house *Muswell Lodge* no longer stands in the vicinity of
Burlington Road's junction with Tetherdown (off
Fortis Green Road). Mr Smith was a nervous householder, given to alarms and spring-guns in the grounds,
but these only persuaded burglars Albert Millsom and
Henry Fowler that the old man must be worth robbing.
They tied him up and he died under their ungentle
questioning. Then they fled to Bath.

But, like rank amateurs, they went a-robbing with a
child's toy bull's-eye lantern and left it behind. It had
belonged to Millsom's young brother-in-law, and when he
was traced Millsom's disappearance explained itself.

In court ruffianly Millsom, thinking that Fowler intended
to turn Queen's Evidence, tried to attack him physically.
Relations between them remained so poor that they were
hanged with William Seaman (p. 36) on the beam between
them.

Westward, five blocks away across the school playing-
fields, **Hertford Road** runs from Durham Road to Finchley
High Road East. Here, in the comfortable suburban residence 'Claymore', Mrs Amelia Sachs ran her baby-farm
(with preliminary mid-wifery and medical attendance) and
used Annie Walters (p. 170) to dispose of the bodies in
Islington.

Half a mile to the north in Friern Barnet, Alfred Arthur
Rouse lived in Buxted Road in 1930. A man with too many
girlfriends and too many impending paternity orders, he
decided that a new life was called for. To this end he drove

his car north, picked up an old tramp as a passenger, killed him in Northamptonshire and set fire to the car. Rouse's plot failed when he saw and addressed two passers-by as he crawled from a ditch near his little inferno. A very skilful technical defence resting on the proposition that the car engine might have caused and fed its own flames was stopped in its tracks when prosecuting counsel Norman Birkett asked the technical expert the coefficient of the expansion of brass. His ignorance of this made him look inadequate in the jury's eyes. And no one has doubted that Rouse was rightly convicted. (Despite the failure of his technique, Sam Furnace (p. 118) imitated it three years later.)

Another shady character from Finchley was Brian Donald Hume, car-dealing spiv, who in 1949 stabbed his fellow fiddler, Stanley Setty, to rob him of a rather paltry sum. Hume lived, and killed Setty, at the flat in the top two storeys of **620b Finchley Road**, and made an extraordinarily fine job of cleaning up the blood and the carpets so that no evidence of Setty's death remained. He was caught because his disposal of the body, though elaborate, was inadequate. He flew it over the Channel in his private plane, and dropped it in parcels into the sea. One drop was made prematurely because of weather conditions, and identifiable remains were washed up.

Even with his sinister flights proven against him, Hume was able to convince the jury that he deserved the benefit of reasonable doubt. He claimed to have disposed of the parcels, contents unknown, for three strange crooks named Greeny, Mac and 'The Boy'. Once acquitted and safe, he admitted that he had invented them and based their descriptions on the detectives who were grilling him.

Then the self-confessed murderer went to live in Switzerland, where he killed again (a taxi-driver). The Swiss, understandably indignant at being forced to give house-room to a pest only at large because of our legal incompetence would still like us to take over from them the expense and responsibility of housing and feeding Hume under lock and key for the rest of his life.

Grahame Young is remembered for poisoning his work-mates with thallium, killing two, at Bovingdon, Herts, in 1971. But he had already spent seven years in Broadmoor for his achievements as a **Neasden** child poisoner.

Grahame had lived with his aunt and uncle at 31 Links Road (running south from the North Circular Road near the Welsh Harp Reservoir) after his mother's death in his infancy. In 1963, when he was thirteen, his father remarried and Grahame was sent to live with him and his new stepmother at **768 North Circular Road**. The boy found the change unsettling. He feared and resented his father's anger, and developed the habit of 'punishing' him with upsetting little doses of antimony whenever he gave him a row. Still greater was his resentment of his stepmother Mollie. If she were out of the way, he reasoned, he would be returned to Links Road. So he killed her with antimony and arsenic.

His know-all nature and the curiosity with which he conducted these poisonings leave the impression that he was something of a misguided scientific experimenter. But comparison with William Allnutt (p. 176) suggests that the wish to escape disciplinary pressure and return to a happier state remembered from early childhood was his real motive.

In 1983 the staid suburbs of Cricklewood and Muswell Hill were placed firmly in the annals of crime by a sedate, homosexual junior civil servant. Dennis Nilsen had been an army chef for several years and a trainee policeman for one before he settled into a clerical job with the DHSS. He rented the front ground-floor flat in **195 Melrose Avenue**, a long 1890s development running west from the junction of Walm Lane with Chichele Road. Here he brought casual sexual partners picked up in central London pubs, especially the Golden Lion in Dean Street, Soho. And here, from Christmas 1978, he occasionally killed them with extraordinary detachment after heavy drinking sessions.

His method was strangulation, usually with a tie. Especially difficult cases were finished off by having their heads held down in basins of cold water. The victims were usually very drunk and very sleepy. Most were dismembered and stored under the floorboards in the flat, where Nilsen masked the stench with disinfectant until he could finally eliminate the remains in midnight garden bonfires, with car tyres to drown the smell of burning flesh.

In this way twelve victims disappeared. The shifting, anonymous nature of the London homosexual demi-monde meant that many were not missed, and those with families or friends to notice their disappearance had already been conducting their lives in a way which made them hard to trace at the best of times. Five of them have still not been identified, even though Nilsen cooperated fully with the police after his arrest.

Seven others were attacked but survived. Some had been so drunk that they doubted their hazy recollection of their host trying to strangle them; some feared that the police would be unsympathetic to them as homosexual drifters. One discovered that Nilsen could easily smother police enquiries by passing off the assault as a lovers' tiff.

In 1981 a developer offered Nilsen £1000 to give up his tenancy. He moved to another converted family house, **23 Cranley Gardens**, on the southwestern slopes of **Muswell Hill**, near Highgate and Queen's Woods. Since his flat was now on the top floor, he vaguely hoped that his compulsive killing would have to end (there being no floorboards for temporary storage and no garden for final cremations). Alas, the compulsion proved too strong. By February 1983 he had killed three more victims, boiling their dismembered limbs and severed heads in a large pot he had previously used for curry-making, and flushing surplus flesh down the lavatory.

His own complaint that the drains were blocked led to his exposure. A plumber found the drains to be full of meat which seemed uncannily human, and Nilsen betrayed his personal concern by moving up and down the stairs all night, working to clear them after the plumber had gone.

His motive remains mysterious, even to himself. There was some sexual element in the compulsion, but happily his disorder is obviously exceptionally rare.

10

Northeast London

It is hard to envisage a region of open countryside stretching from Finsbury Fields through Pentonville, Canonbury, Barnsbury and Highbury to Finsbury Park. The Angel is no longer a pub. Islington High Street seems simply the busier end of Upper Street. Small clothing factories and workshops are scattered among the streets to the north of City Road and Goswell Road. Restored traditional terraces mark the gentrification of Barnsbury and Canonbury. Varying experiments in types of council housing ramble northwest off the Essex Road. It is a mixed, busy, interesting area.

The crime of Thomas Cooper, however, points to the rural nature of north Islington 150 years ago. This 22-year-old Clerkenwell bricklayer turned footpad infested Hornsey Wood (in today's Finsbury Park) in 1842. On May 5th PC Charles Moss located him near the Hornsey Wood Tavern, a favourite country refreshment house of the time (close to today's boating pond). Cooper shot and wounded Moss, which attracted the attention of another policeman, PC Mallett, and a journeyman baker called Mott, who was walking in the woods. These two gave chase and Cooper fired at them, wounding Mott in the shoulder before racing off toward Highbury.

Another baker, named Mr Howard, was driving his chaise down the Hornsey Road. He saw the commotion in the distance and drove after Cooper who was making for

Highbury Barn (in today's Blackstock Road). Another
policeman, called Timothy Daly, closed in on him, and
near Highbury Cottage Cooper jumped over a hedge and
found himself in a short cul-de-sac called *Black Ditch*,
bounded by a paling fence. As he backed against the fence,
Daly and Howard advanced to seize him. Cooper fired
both his large horse pistols. Daly was killed instantly:
Howard was uninjured, and seized Cooper with the aid of
two gardeners.

The dense murder area of Islington lies further south, in
the back streets behind Upper Street and the City Road.
Danbury Street lies about four blocks east of Camden
Passage, parallel with Upper Street. Here at no 11 the
very stupid Annie Walters lodged with a policeman. She
purported to be a short-stay foster-parent, looking after
babies briefly before handing them over to permanent
adoptive parents. Her sentimental manner deceived her
landlady, though there was a puzzling occasion when Mrs
Walters left a 'dear little girl' to have her nappy changed,
and the change revealed a dear little boy.

Stranger still were her stories of fantastically wealthy
and noble adopters who took babies from her in the streets,
clasped them in their bejewelled hands, and drove them
away to lives of luxury. At length the policeman landlord
conferred with another policeman neighbour, and the two
agreed that the streetside adoptions seemed unlikely. Mrs
Walters was followed in her ramblings with a baby, and
eventually was found to be carrying its corpse to some
fairly deserted refuse tips in Whitechapel. One of her
baby's feeding bottles was filled with lethal chlorodyne.
Investigations in the notorious Flower and Dean Street
vicinity showed that Mrs Walters was a familiar figure in
the public houses there, carrying expiring infants. And

Mrs Walters' own stupid excuses led back to Mrs Amelia Sachs.

Twenty-five years younger than Mrs Walters, and far more able and presentable, Mrs Sachs ran a thriving business as an accoucheuse in East Finchley. Her trim suburban house had been converted into a small private lying-in hospital. Mrs Sachs herself nursed and midwived, and negotiated with the doctor to attend to difficult cases.

But the real appeal of her business was that the babies could be left with her permanently. Unlike Mrs Dyer (p. 163) she made sure that the girls leaving their 'shameful bundles' expected – nay, wanted! – never to see or hear of them again. This whole sordid trade comprised layer after layer of hypocritical eye-closing. Social morality forbade recognition of the fact that healthy sexual appetite might find expression outside marriage, and so pregnant girls were forced to look for a discreet midwife-cum-adoption agency. The girls did not want to know that their babies might come to a bad end in Mrs Sachs's hands, and so they did not ask any searching questions. Mrs Sachs did not want to know exactly how the babies were got rid of, and so she employed Mrs Walters to take them away to Islington. There the chlorodyne bottle supplied the squalid end to the myth of female 'purity'.

Little time was wasted in putting Mrs Sachs and Mrs Walters out of sight and out of mind. They were arrested in late November 1902 and hanged in January 1903, with none of the usual squeamishness about hanging women.

Not far from Danbury Street, Colebrook Row runs from City Road to St Peter's Street. Tucked in behind it, paralleling Camden Passage, lies Duncan Terrace. Rosina Field, a prostitute working the area, lodged there at no 13 in the 1930s. Fred Murphy lived at 57a Colebrook Row. Harding's furniture warehouse where he worked was around the corner at **22 Islington Green**, the triangle at the junction of Essex Road with Upper Street. Messrs Harding were surprised when Murphy reported finding a dead woman in the warehouse and then disappeared for a day.

He turned up at Poplar police station, where he told of having been on a pub crawl during the time in which Rosina Field had been killed. But his clothes were blood-stained and he had been seen sneaking into 22 Islington Green with Miss Field at a time when he claimed to have been drinking elsewhere.

Moreover this was the second time Murphy had been the last person seen with a murdered tart. 'Carbolic Kate' Peck had been spotted in his company in Aldgate shortly before she was discovered with her throat cut. Murphy escaped prosecution on that occasion because the main witness against him disappeared. He was not so lucky this time, and was executed for Rosina Field's murder.

Noel Road runs from Colebrook Row across Danbury Street. In the 1960s Joe Orton, one of the finest post-war English playwrights, shared a flat there with his friend Keith Halliwell.

Orton and Halliwell were irrepressible young homosexuals with literary ambitions. They had seen Orton's talent reach fruition and recognition in the swinging 'sixties. Orton used the external forms of traditional farce. But he exploited the licence of the times to push its sexual extravagance beyond the limitations of the commercial West End. And he used the traditional mainsprings of farce – lust and avarice – to make a bleak comment on the emptiness and loneliness of human existence.

As Orton's fame grew it became apparent that Halliwell would never match his talent. Homosexual circles still welcomed Joe's 'friend'. But the 'straight' establishment of culture was less willing to accept a young man with more pretensions than ability who was not a traditional wife. Orton felt social pressure to break off the relationship. Halliwell felt intense pressures of jealousy and frustration.

It exploded in August 1967, when Halliwell battered Orton to death and then stabbed himself. It would be an ordinary domestic murder, with the commonplace motive of possessive jealousy, were not the victim a brilliant writer and the household homosexual.

Until a few years ago an old tin kettle, painted blue, hung outside a yard entry on the south side of Islington High Street, near the Angel. In the 1950s and '60s this marked a pleasant little teashop called *The Blue Kettle*. Its peace was marred by a fight in 1955, when a national serviceman drinking a cup of tea made some disparaging remarks about the teddy boy costumes of other young men in the café. By instant agreement he went out to fight in the yard with one of them – 'Nicky the Greek' Xinaris. But Xinaris was carrying a knife. He drew it when the fight went against him. The soldier was killed, and Xinaris helped give teddy boys a bad name, as though young men hadn't been scrapping and resorting to knives all over East London for a century.

East of Islington lie the northern adjuncts of the East End: Haggerston, Kingsland and Dalston. **Ashwin Street** is a short unlovely road running off Dalston Lane opposite the old Dalston Junction Station. Save for a garage on its west side and peeling tarmac over its cobbles it has changed little since 1882, when the large bare brick **Shiloh Pentecostal Church** at the Beech Street (now Abbott Street) end was a Baptist chapel.

Reeves' water colours factory glared down Ashwin Street

from Beech Street, and in those days a Turkish Bath stood beside it.

P.C. George Cole looked up the street one foggy December night and wondered which of these three institutions a suspicious loiterer in a soft felt hat was 'casing'. He took him in charge, and led him down the street as far as the Railway Tavern on the Dalston Lane corner (the bookmaker's today) where the prisoner broke away and ran back toward Beech Street. He paused at a low railing, still fronting the space between the chapel steps and the garage, where Cole grappled with him. After a fierce struggle in the street, three shots rang out. The first two chipped doorway brickwork and a gutterpipe in houses opposite; the third left P.C. Cole dying on the chapel steps. The assailant disappeared down Beech Street leaving his hat in the roadway.

Among the people running, too late, to Cole's assistance was a young man named Evans who came out of the Railway Tavern and was asked to go for a doctor.

Two years later Evans testified in court that he and a youth named Miles had passed the evening with Thomas Henry Orrock, drinking in a large number of pubs between The Eaglet in Bridport Place and the Walford in Stoke Newington Road, and planning to rob the chapel.

The spree ended in the Railway Tavern where Orrock left his friends and went over the road into the building. A meeting was in progress, but Orrock was a regular attender at Bible classes, so his presence aroused no suspicion. He knew the premises contained money and valuable sacramental plate, and preparatory to stealing this he slipped downstairs and unlocked a window opening on the recess where he was later arrested. And outside, in a niche still visible in the recess wall, he hid two chisels and a wedge.

After the murder these tools were found. One chisel had

the word ROCK crudely scratched on it. Later inspection was to prove that this had been altered from ORROCK. It was the identification Mrs Preston of City Road had put on it when it was left with her for grinding.

In 1884 the police had a complete case when Evans, gaoled for theft, confessed his part. Miles confirmed the story, and told how he and a youth called Mortimer had gone to Tottenham Marshes where Orrock showed them a pistol he had bought and fired a bullet into a tree halfway between the Ferry Boat Inn and the River Lea Bridge. The bullet was still there, and matched that taken from Cole's head.

It took the jury twenty minutes to find Orrock guilty. He was only 21 when he was hanged.

At the southeast corner of Finsbury Park, where Green Lanes crosses Seven Sisters Road, stands the huge barn of the Manor House pub, where, according to his several and frequently retracted confessions, Peter Louis Alphon was briefed to carry out the intimidation which resulted in the A6 murder for which James Hanratty was hanged. On the night after Michael Gregsten's murder, Alphon was staying at the Alexandra Court Hotel (now replaced by the modern office premises of the Alexandra National Housing Association) on the corner of Seven Sisters Road and Queen's Drive where his sleepless behaviour over the next week disturbed a fellow-guest, who drew it to the attention of the police.

When Bethnal Green, Mile End and Bow declined, the more prosperous senior clerks and small businessmen of East London moved into new nineteenth-century developments to the north. Hackney spread from Bethnal Green to the marshes where the River Lea oozed slowly south before passing through the East End to join the Thames at

Canning Town. The rather characterless suburbia of Clapton led north from Hackney to Stamford Hill, and to the west adjoined Stoke Newington – a village three miles north of London in Defoe's day, a continuation of the built-up Shoreditch-Kingsland-Dalston road north from Bishopsgate by the 1850s.

In 1847 **Grove Place, Hackney** was a block of houses at the corner where Grahame Road now joins Mare Street (the main street of Hackney). An old man named Samuel Nelme lived there with his daughter, whose husband had died of delirium tremens two years previously. The old gentleman was severe with his twelve-year-old grandson, William Allnutt and beat him. The lad came to hate and fear him. After a severe beating in October William discovered arsenic stored in the house and added it liberally to the sugar his grandfather took in his tea. The old man died five days later, but the cause and the doctored sugar were quickly discovered. William confessed, and stood trial for murder. The judge went out of his way to comment that the crime was a monstrous and unfilial act of villainy, and almost regretted that he could no longer order a child to hang.

The first railway murder was a Hackney event. The victim, an elderly head bank clerk, lived at 5 Clapton Square. (Its solidly prosperous terraced neighbours still stand, just north of the termination of Mare Street). Mr Thomas Briggs dined every Saturday with his married niece at her home in 23 Nelson Square (today's Furley Road), Peckham.

Another Hackney resident also visited south London in July 1864. Franz Müller, a German tailor, lodged at 16 Park Terrace, part of today's Old Ford Road opposite Victoria Park. He passed the early evening of Saturday

July 9th visiting a prostitute in Peckham, and returned to Hackney on the same train – indeed, in the same compartment – from Fenchurch Street as Mr Briggs.

At Hackney Wick station Müller left the train unnoticed, and two young clerks who entered the compartment found its seats sticky with blood. They alerted the guard, and Mr Briggs's unconscious body was soon discovered on the line between Bow and Hackney. He never recovered. His watch and chain were missing. A hat that was not his remained in the compartment.

A Cheapside jeweller named John Death quickly came forward with Mr Briggs's watch-chain, which he had exchanged for cheap jewellery on the Monday following the murder. Nine days later a cabman named Matthews realized that a cardboard box Müller had given his little girl to play with bore Death's imprint, and he too went to the police. There he identified the hat found in Mr Brigg's compartment. It was a short top-hat (of modern size, rather than the Victorian stovepipe) which Müller had seen and liked in the window of Walker's hat shop, Crawford Street, Marylebone, and which Matthews had collected for him.

Müller had gone. Not, apparently, fled for he had long previously given notice to his landlord and declared his intention of emigrating to America. But Mr Briggs's watch and chain, it seemed, had supplied the funds for his steerage passage.

Müller was crossing the Atlantic on the sailing ship *Victoria*. The police took Matthews and Death on a fast steamship and reached New York before him. When Müller was arrested he was found to have retained Mr Briggs's hat and cut it down to the new size he favoured. For several years such hats were called 'Müller cut-downs'. His execution at Newgate was accompanied by a good deal

of uninterrupted mugging in the crowd, which contributed
to the case for abolishing public hanging a few years later.

Arthur Hosein ran a trouser-making factory in Mare Street,
Hackney, in 1969. He was an able and energetic young
Trinidadian Asian who had worked his way up from
employed hand to entrepreneur, and brought his weaker
and more dependent younger brother, Nizamodeen, over
to England to share the success he was enjoying.

Arthur was flamboyantly ambitious. He bought Rooks
Farm at Stocking Pelham in Essex, and then found that he
lacked the means to support his pose as a country squire.
So the brothers contrived an outrageous scheme to kidnap
the wife of newspaper proprietor Rupert Murdoch and
hold her to ransom.

Their own incompetence led them to trail the company's
directorial Rolls Royce to Wimbledon at a time when Mr
Murdoch was out of the country, and so inadvertently
kidnap Mrs Muriel McKay, wife of the *News of the World's*
deputy chairman from her home in Arthur Road, Wimbledon (p. 226). They fluffed repeated attempts to collect the
ransom money. Their blue Volvo car was spotted at pick-
up points from time to time, and only disagreements
between the newspapermen involved and the police as to
the best method of pursuing Britain's first mercenary
kidnappers delayed their arrest. Mrs McKay has never
been seen again, and the Hoseins, though convicted and
imprisoned, have never confessed. It is assumed that they
murdered her in Essex, and rumoured that they disposed
of the remains by feeding them to the farm pigs.

Stoke Newington's elegant eighteenth-century houses cry
out for restoration and preservation in their surrounding
sea of dull Victorian terraces. In one of these drab roads
Louise Masset established a unique position in the history

of infanticide. The 33-year-old French piano teacher murdered her four-year-old son because he was an inconvenience to her love-life.

Under happer circumstances one might rejoice at Louise as evidence of warm passions unsuppressed by the heavy yellow-brick semi-detached lodging-house respectability of **29 Bethune Road** (between Manor Road and Amhurst Park) where she boarded in 1903. Louise was unmarried, but had a son, flamboyantly named 'Manfred'. She was pursuing an affair with Eudore Lucas, a student who lived next door.

Manfred was safely out of the way in Tottenham, where Louise had boarded him. But even so he seemed an encumbrance to a permanent liaison with Eudore, whose ardour was cooling. Louise decided on desperate measures.

She collected Manfred, explaining that his father was going to take over his upbringing in France. She was seen with him on London Bridge Station. Three hours afterwards Manfred's naked body was found in the ladies' lavatory at the recently demolished *Dalston Junction station* accompanied by the heavy stone which had been used to batter him to death. Two days later his clothes were found in the waiting room at Brighton – where Louise had spent the weekend in the company of Eudore.

Louise told an unlikely story of having registered the boy to enter a new children's home that two ladies had told her they were opening in Chelsea and handing him over to them at London Bridge. Of course no such ladies were traced. And the murderous stone had come from the garden of 29 Bethune Road. Even today heavy lumps of gritstone neatly border the laurels and a hollybush in this little garden.

It is rare for presentable young women to be hanged without protest, but Mlle Masset went far beyond offending

Victorian sexual mores. She outraged maternity and died unlamented.

Walthamstow and Leyton are dull late nineteenth-century developments, east of the River Lea and to the south of Epping Forest. Edgar Edwards of 89 Church Road, Leyton, was a farsighted, thrifty, enterprising late Victorian petit-bourgeois thief, with a Wellsian interest in small shops. Seemingly he fitted his environment perfectly. But he was anything but dull.

Away down south in Camberwell, John and Beatrice Darby had decided to give up their small grocery at *22* **Wyndham Road** (a few shops from the period still stand at the western end of the road). The advertisement of their business for sale caught Mr Edwards' eye in 1902, and he went down to investigate.

Recognizing a bargain, he took the contents, but not the premises. Since he also took the bodies of the Darbies and their baby, he took it as a gift rather than a purchase. He thriftily removed the Darby family by the same cart that carried away their stocks, and prudently posted a notice advertising that the business had been sold.

Back in Leyton he dismembered the family and buried them in his garden. Like George Joseph Smith (p. 154) he had devised a discreet and profitable mode of murder, and it might even have borne successful repetition.

But Mr Edwards' next attempt failed. When he violently attacked another grocer whose business was for sale, his victim resisted. Questions led to evasions. The bodies were found in his garden; and a most ingenious form of crime had been nipped in the bud.

George Woolf was merely nasty. A Hoxton lad (p. 30), he took up with local girl Charlotte Cheeseman during the Boer War while her acknowledged sweetheart was fighting in South Africa. When the young soldier came home there was trouble. Woolf skulked out of the way until it was clear that Charlotte had been dropped for associating with him. Then he sneaked back.

But Charlotte became pregnant, and pressed for marriage. Woolf now behaved disgustingly. He wrote her a cruel brush-off letter; and he wrote to the cigar-maker she worked for accusing her of dishonesty at work.

Still Charlotte hoped desperately for reconciliation and marriage. On January 25th Woolf took her for a drink in the Rosemary Branch at Hoxton. From there they went north to Tottenham, and were seen together on the bridge over the railway between Northumberland Park and Tottenham Hale. The next day Charlotte's body was found in a ditch on the way back to **Scotland Green** and Tottenham High Road. She had been battered to death with a chisel.

Woolf tried to escape by enlisting in the army. It did not save him: he was hanged.

A little further south on Tottenham High Road an anarchist named Paul Hefeld and his comrade 'Jacob' – whose surname may have been Lepidus – launched one of the most extraordinary Keystone Kops-fashion incidents ever to take place on London's streets. The two had worked at a factory in Chesnut Road, and on a Saturday morning in 1908 they waited at the gate to snatch the wages from the cashier who delivered them.

With a nearby policeman racing after them and summoning assistance, they raced down Chesnut Road, turned north across Scales Road and up Dawlish Road into **Mitchley Road**. There, beside the Mission Hall, Hefeld shot PC Tyler and also a twelve-year-old boy, Ralph Joscelyne, who was running for cover behind a motor-car the police had requisitioned.

These were, in fact, the only two murders committed by the 'Tottenham Anarchists', though in the course of the morning they fired a further 400 rounds, and injured a large number of people.

The chase continued along Park View Road, and over the railway to the marshes, compelling the police to follow on foot. They ran northwards until they could round Lockwood Reservoir, making for Billet Road. Then, realizing that police reinforcements were awaiting them there, they continued east across Walthamstow Avenue to Chingford Road.

On Chingford Road they hi-jacked a southbound tram. Almost all the passengers leapt off as they entered, guns blazing, and the driver hid under a seat. The conductor (at gunpoint) showed them how to drive it, and the frustrated police commandeered a milk van to keep up the pursuit and gunfight. The anarchists shot the pony.

Resolutely, the police halted a tram going the other way; threw it into reverse and clanged down Chingford Road, shooting at their quarry.

The conductor of the thieves' tram astutely improvised a warning that a police trap was awaiting them around the bend in Walthamstow at Forest Road. Suspicious, but not risking a challenge, they leapt off the tram and ran north up Fulbourne Road to Winchester Road. Where the River Ching ran across the road and allowed a break in the railway blocking the eastern approaches of Epping Forest, they left the main road and headed across country for Hale End. But the newly built cottages at what is now Oak Crescent halted them. Hefeld shot Lepidus, who was almost all-in after the chase, and then ran into a cottage and up the stairs, where he shot himself as the police pounded up after him.

North of Tottenham lies Edmonton, and north of Edmonton, Southgate. Here, in 1948, at the garage entrance to **112 Wades Hill**, Donald George Thomas, an army deserter, shot PC N. Edgar. It was a straightforward case of murder resisting arrest. Thomas retreated to South London, where he and his mistress Mrs Winkless boarded at Mrs Smeed's in Stockwell. He was arrested there, and would be almost forgotten had he not been uniquely reprieved from execution for the murder of a policeman because Parliament was (unsuccessfully) attempting abolition at the time.

11

– From Bermondsey to Battersea –

Across the river from the City of London lies the borough that was for centuries effectually the second largest city in England: the Borough of the South Works of London Bridge, or Southwark. Borough High Street runs directly from London Bridge.

In 1197 two tycoons swopped a pair of manors from their real estate portfolios. The Archbishop of Canterbury accepted Lambeth, on the Thames bank about a mile west of the Borough, in exchange for Dartford. On reflection he decided to use it as his town house instead of adding it to his investments. Southwark innkeeping profited by the increase of travel between Canterbury and London.

Along the Bankside between east Lambeth and Southwark, the Bishops of Rochester and Winchester bought properties which their successors leased out. In Henry VIII's reign, Rochester's cook, Richard Ross, poisoned the soup at a banquet, and became the sole victim of Henry's new penalty for poisoners. He was boiled alive.

Meanwhile Winchester's property had become notorious for its brothels. The holiday nature of the Bankside was increased by the bear-baiting ring, the theatres, and the first of the south bank pleasure gardens. Until the coming of the railways, such features encouraged the presence of a criminal demi-monde in Southwark and Lambeth, living in slum areas around Mint Street ('the Mint') and south of Union Street ('Alsatia').

Eastwards, leatherworkers centred on Bermondsey. The drawback to tanning is that it stinks. No one who could afford not to do so would willingly live near a tannery. Bermondsey quickly developed atrocious slums and by the 1840s Jacob's Island was the worst in London. It was from the south bank slums that the great nineteenth-century cholera epidemics sprang.

With the arrival of the railways, Waterloo station dominated East Lambeth and dragged down that residential neighbourhood. The riverside became a dismal region of dirty warehouses.

Squalid Bermondsey inevitably witnessed much of the violence attendant upon overcrowding and deprivation. The most horrible nineteenth-century infanticide took place in the *Old King's Head Tavern* in *Greenbank*, **Tooley Street**, a little court just west of Shipwright's Court and the Shipwright's Arms where parts of London Bridge station offices are now. Edward Dwyer was a work-shy brush salesman with a taste for violence. In 1843 he finished a well-earned sentence for grievous bodily harm (he had bitten out a section of an opponent's cheek). Once free, he put in a hard day's drinking at the seedy pub, starting at three in the afternoon. At nine in the evening, his wife and mother-in-law came in and roundly abused him in front of his friends. They slapped him, and left him to look after his three-month-old baby. Dwyer put it on the street until his friends persuaded him to fetch it in from the cold.

He made an oracular drunken remark to no one in particular. 'Blood on a brick', he said, 'would look very funny. Blood on the wall would look queer. If a bullock's head was beat against the wall there would be plenty of blood on it.'

Then, before anybody could stop him, he picked up the baby by its thigh and smashed its head on the bar counter.

Frederick and Maria Manning were Bermondsey's most
notorious Victorian murderers. She was a handsome raven-
haired Swiss, born Maria De Roux. Patrick O'Connor, a
London Docks exciseman with a surprisingly large nest-
egg, had been Manning's rival for her hand in 1845. He
had persuaded the Mannings, after they married, to take
the tenancy of a pub in Shoreditch. When that failed,
Maria felt that O'Connor owed them compensation.

By 1849 she was visiting him at his lodgings in Greenwood Place off the Mile End Road, and urging him to visit
their new house, *3 Minver* or *Minerva Place, New Weston
Street, Bermondsey*. This was the southern end of **Weston
Street**, south of Long Lane. The terrace of cottages on the
west were entered from their western faces, hence the
address was Minver Place rather than New Weston Street.

O'Connor was nervous about visiting cholera-ridden
Bermondsey. The Mannings exploited this fear by serving
him brandy as a prophylactic (he was a notoriously light
drinker) and getting him to sign a transfer of some railway
stock to them. Their full intentions could not be realized at
this first visit as a Mr Walsh was also present, and saw the
unsteady O'Connor safely home.

To persuade him to make a second visit, the Mannings
pretended that their lodger, a medical student, was being
visited by his sister and wanted a change of company and
a special dinner for her. On the pretext of smartening
himself up for the sister, O'Connor was persuaded to start
down the basement stairs to the kitchen. Maria put her
arm around his neck as he reached the bottom step and
fired a pistol into his head. Frederick then came downstairs
and found him moaning. Later Manning remarked, 'I
never really liked him, and I battered his head with a
ripping chisel.'

Once O'Connor was definitely dead, the couple stripped
him, tied his legs back in a neat bundle, and buried him in

–

the grave Maria had prepared in their tiny kitchen. Maria cleaned the place up thoroughly the next day, enlisting the aid of a twelve-year-old orphan selling matches on the street. (In addition to her 5d pay, the orphan made off with an egg, a razor, a purse and a pair of stockings.)

Thereafter the Mannings separated, each trying to cheat the other. Frederick went to a furniture dealer to sell all their property. When he returned, Maria had already removed hers and disappeared. She had gone to O'Connor's lodgings and stolen cash, two gold watches, and a quantity of continental railway stock. With these she absconded to Edinburgh.

O'Connor's friends and fellow-workers at London Dock missed him and soon learned that he had last been seen at the Mannings' home – where, on investigation, the police found the grave and the body.

Maria was caught in Edinburgh when she tried to sell the shares. Frederick was a little harder to trace: he had gone to Jersey.

In custody they tried to blame each other. Maria retained an icy self-control during the trial, but burst into impassioned abuse of England and its justice when the judge sentenced her, and threw bits of ruc, which were strewed on the dock, at him. This ended the traditional practice of 'sweetening' the court with herbs. And because she wore black bombazine for her execution the demand for that popular material fell abruptly.

Cross Street, Southwark, ran west from Blackfriars Road in 1806, being rebuilt in a terrace of rather tall artisan's cottages as **Meymott Street** later in the century. Elderly widowed Mrs Ann Maria Pooley kept her savings in her little house here. The fact was known locally, and a labourer called John Maycock persuaded John Pope to help him steal it. They went to Mrs Pooley's cottage after dark and broke in by removing bricks from near the door, so that a hand thrust in could pull the bolt back. Once in, they replaced the bricks and nobody noticed the difference, rotten housing fabric being common in the area.

Inside they found themselves trapped in a small scullery whose door into the house was locked. So, to Pope's terror, they waited out the night. When Mrs Pooley came out in the morning Maycock throttled her, and the two ransacked the house, finding £90.

This was a fortune to them, and their sudden acquisition of wealth was not forgotten when, a few weeks later, puzzled acquaintances made their way in to Mrs Pooley's house to see where she was – and found her so decomposed that the cause of death could not be guessed. Pope and Maycock were questioned.

The constables extracted a confession from Pope by implying that he would not be charged if he incriminated Maycock. The trial judge was outraged when he heard this, and directed the jury to acquit Pope. Maycock was less lucky, and hanged.

A year later, in 1807, an unsolved murder took place where **Webber Street** (then called *Higgler's Lane*) **meets Great Suffolk Street** (then called *Dirty Lane* – by all accounts aptly). Southwark Bridge Road had not yet been constructed to dominate the junction.

Elizabeth Winterflood was known to her London acquaintance as Ann Webb. She was a prostitute, but every one acknowledged that she was a lady of the highest character. Her landlady and neighbours saw her out looking for trade after midnight near the junction one August night, but at 2.45 A.M. a passer-by found her lying at the end of Higgler's Lane where the costers' barrows were parked. Her posture was indecent, her white dress pulled up above her waist and her legs splayed. When he went to

–

arouse what he assumed was a lewd drunk, he found her to be dead.

A doctor from Blackfriars Road found it difficult to ascertain the cause of death in the darkness. He totally overlooked her horrible mutilation until a search under the nearby carts which turned up her velvet shoes and bonnet also revealed a piece of flesh, which turned out to have been chopped off her genitals.

The doctor saw that the mutilation would not in itself have killed her and decided that she had been strangled with a strip of cloth that was found nearby.

Elizabeth's former boyfriend was suspected. Thomas Greenaway ('Weeping Billy') passed himself off as a carpenter under the name of William White, but was actually a ponce, known to have quarrelled with Elizabeth recently when she refused to support him. She had also threatened suicide because of his infidelities. Another girl in his stable, it was rumoured, had in fact drowned herself from jealousy.

Several people testified to seeing White/Greenaway with Elizabeth or in the vicinity just before and just after her death. But some of them, especially the girl's landlady, were unduly hostile to him. The judge warned the jury against possible biased witnesses, and Greenaway was acquitted. He seems to have been extremely lucky, though if he did commit the murder he would be an unusual instance of a sexual mutilator exercising his perversion on a habitual sexual partner.

Two classic poisoners, both rumoured to have been Jack the Ripper, were associated with the south bank. Thomas Neill Cream was a cross-eyed doctor who first lived in the area in 1876 as a post-graduate medical student at St Thomas's Hospital. In 1878 he went home to Canada and quickly made a foul reputation for himself. He practised as an abortionist rather than a healer, and one of his patients was found dead in the privy outside his office, poisoned by chloroform. It seemed likely that she had been brutally forced to swallow it but there was not enough evidence to bring charges.

In 1880 another patient died, this time as a result of her abortion. Again Cream could not be charged.

In 1881 Cream was marketing a quack remedy for epilepsy and merrily committing adultery with a patient's wife. To make life more convenient all round, he added a good dose of strychnine to the husband's epilepsy cure, and everyone was satisfied that the unfortunate Mr Scott had died of natural syncope during one of his fits.

Then Cream first displayed his incomprehensible craving to write incriminatory letters. He wrote to the coroner and the District Attorney complaining that the druggist making up Mr Scott's prescription had overdone the strychnine. Exhumation revealed the poison, and Cream was sentenced to a long spell in Joliet Prison.

In 1891 his family secured his release, and he came back to England, now calling himself 'Dr Neill' to his patients and 'Fred' to the prostitutes of the triangle between Lambeth Bridge, Blackfriars Bridge and St George's Circus. (Apart from a couple of pubs, all the addresses in Cream's criminal career have been swept away in road-widening or redevelopment, or have had their nature and character changed.) He stayed, first at the Anderton Hotel, 162–165 Fleet Street (on the north side, just east of Dr Johnson's Court). From this convenient location he picked up Elizabeth Masters in Ludgate Circus, and had a drink with her in the King Lud. He went back to her rooms at 9 Orient Buildings, Hercules Road, Lambeth, and found her services sufficiently satisfying to make another appointment.

In the meantime he took lodgings at 103 Lambeth Palace Road. In the York Hotel at the corner of York Road and Waterloo Road, he met Ellen Donworth, and went back to her rooms at 8 Duke Street (today's Duchy Street). He was seen leaving her house a couple of hours before she collapsed on the pavement opposite the **Duke of Wellington** in **Waterloo Road**. 'Fred' had given her poison. Unfortunately the police knew another Fred of Miss Donworth's acquaintance, and went looking for the wrong man.

Cream promptly wrote two of his barmy letters: one signed 'H.W.B.' purported to be a warning to Ellen Donworth that the heir of W.H. Smith the bookseller intended to poison her, and the other, to Smith himself – enclosing the 'warning' – offered 'H. Bayne's' services as a barrister.

Elizabeth Masters was looking out of her window with a friend at the time of her appointment with Cream, and to their great amusement they spotted him lecherously following another strumpet called Matilda Clover. She had attracted his attention at the Canterbury Arms in Upper Marsh (unmarked today: the roadway through the housing estate at the northeast corner between Lambeth Palace Road and Westminster Bridge Road). Giggling, Elizabeth and her friend put on their bonnets and followed Cream and Matilda at a little distance till they saw him go into her lodgings at 27 **Lambeth Road**. Clearly he would not be coming as arranged to Hercules Road.

But Elizabeth was lucky. It was Matilda who was offered, and accepted, one of 'Fred's' capsules and died in agony that night. Her doctor assumed that he was dealing with a case of delirium tremens, as she was notoriously alcoholic, and Cream could have escaped unsuspected again. But he made sure that poison was considered by writing to Lady Russell at the Savoy Hotel, accusing Lord Russell of murdering Matilda; and he wrote a quasi-blackmailing letter to the distinguished Dr William Broadbent accusing him. Both letters purported to be from a detective offering to clear the 'murderers' of suspicion.

In January 1892 Cream made a quick trip to Canada, where he had five hundred flysheets printed, addressed to the guests at the Metropole Hotel, warning them that the killer of Ellen Donworth was on the hotel staff and their lives were in danger. The printed signature was W.H. Murray: the flysheets were never used.

In three months he was back in London, staying at Edwards Hotel, 14–15 Euston Square. At the Alhambra in Leicester Square, one of the great Victorian 'beats', he picked up Louise Harris who, in compliment to the young man she lived with, called herself Lou Harvey. They went, by her account, to 'a hotel' at the Oxford Street end of Berwick Street to pass the night. This was probably the Green Man at no 57, or just possibly an unmarked house of accommodation over a shop.

Lou was street-smart. When she met Cream by appointment on the embankment the following night, she pretended to accept the capsule he gave her but threw it away. Emma Shrivell and Alice Marsh, both lodging at *118* **Stamford Street**, Lambeth, were less fortunate and died together in convulsions.

This time Cream's accusatory letters came too close to home and were traced. Walter Harper had lodged at 103 Lambeth Palace Road while completing his medical studies. When Cream wrote (as 'W. H. Murray') to Harper's father in Barnstaple accusing the young man of the Stamford Street murders, and enclosing a cutting on Ellen Donworth, attention was drawn to the cross-eyed fellow-lodger who matched one description of Donworth's killer. Cream was swiftly arrested and, apparently to his surprise, convicted.

His last words, as the drop fell under him, are supposed to have been, 'I am Jack the – ' He was not. He was quite definitely in prison in America throughout 1888 and 1889.

–

On the other hand, George Chapman, under his real name of Severin Klosowski, was working as a hairdresser's assistant in or around the White Hart, Whitechapel High Street, right in the Ripper territory throughout 1888. But he was no driven maniac. Like Daniel Good (p. 223) Klosowski seems to have been hopelessly incapable of bringing a romantic relationship to a clean end.

As a Polish immigrant, he 'married' Lucy Baderski of Walthamstow, whom he met in a Polish club in Clerkenwell. It was embarrassing, then, when another woman arrived from Poland claiming to be Mrs Klosowski. This imbroglio was settled in Lucy's favour, and in 1891 the couple emigrated to America.

A year later Klosowski returned alone (without having killed Lucy). He took up with a woman named Annie Chapman, lived with her for a year, adopted her surname, and claimed to be an American. (He may have hoped to distance himself from the Polish Jews of London, he being a gentile Catholic.)

In 1895 he settled to living with railwayman Shadrach Spink's estranged wife, Mary. They claimed to be married (it would, of course, have been bigamy on both sides) and moved to Hastings where Chapman set up as a barber and Mary played the piano while he wielded the razor. These 'musical shaves' were popular, but Mary's increasing drunkenness was tiresome. Shadrach had simply left her because of it. Chapman bought some tartar emetic . . .'

The pair returned to London, where Chapman found his final metier as a publican. He took the licence of the *Prince of Wales* in **Bartholomew Square, off Old Street**. (None of Chapman's London pubs still stand.) Here Mrs Chapman fell sick and, at the end of 1895, died.

In 1898 Chapman 'married' Bessie Taylor. By all accounts she was the most prepossessing and ladylike of his various 'wives', and English observers later expressed themselves mystified by his attraction for her. Since photographs show him as a dark, lively, virile figure, and Bessie may not have shared xenophobia common in her society, their bewilderment seems misplaced. What we really don't know is why Chapman tired of her. They spent a year managing The Grapes in Bishop's Stortford, then in 1900 took *The Monument Tavern*, **Union Street, Lambeth**. This did not survive Chapman's management. Widowed once again (Bessie died in February, 1901), with his lease about to fall in, Chapman suffered an opportune fire. The insurance company believed it to be arson, and refused to compensate him.

Undeterred, Chapman took the licence of *The Crown* at *213* **Borough High Street** (where the post office is today). He advertised for a new barmaid, and in the short run was highly satisfied with Maud Marsh. Her family were less certain about the live-in post, despite Mr Chapman's mendacious assurance that another family lodged in the building. Her mother was horrified when Maud wrote asking for advice now that Mr Chapman proposed paying her £35 (presumably her year's wages) and sending her home if she wouldn't let him have his wicked will of her. Nor was Mrs Marsh reassured by a second, calmer letter, saying that Maud regretted the first one; she was now engaged to Mr Chapman and very happy. Finally Maud reported herself secretly 'married' in such a hurry that there had been no time for a family wedding.

But the young girl's shamelessness hardly deserved to prove fatal within a year. This time the doctor was suspicious: this was the second Mrs Chapman he had treated for similar symptoms in the space of twenty months. All three Mrs Chapmans were exhumed, and their bodies found to be in that excellent state of preservation characteristic of antimony poisoning. Chapman was caught.

Ex-inspector Abberline said to Inspector Godley, 'I see

you got Jack the Ripper at last'. He and Godley had
participated in the house-to-house interrogations with
which the police had blanketed Whitechapel in 1888, and
Klosowski's Lucy had told them of some very mysterious
nocturnal absences on her husband's part. We don't know,
of course, whether Abberline's remark was mildly teasing.
Psychologically Chapman was quite different from the
Ripper – who seemed to fear the attraction a woman's
body held for him, whereas Chapman seemed to fear the
anger and resentment consequent on ending a relationship
openly. The two used consistent and different methods.
Abberline may have been confusing Klosowski with a
rather similarly named Pole believed (quite possibly correctly) by Sir Robert Anderson to have been the Ripper,
and noted as a plausible suspect by Sir Melville
MacNaghten.

Before the private houses in **York Road** were swept away,
Mrs Mabel Edmunds kept a lodging house at *no 156,* **next
to County Hall**. Among the residents was her young
nephew Frederick Maximilian Jesse, a gardener whose
industry did not satisfy his aunt. One Saturday afternoon
in July 1923 she berated his idleness and upset him by
raking up family differences. Not content with words, she
beat him with a broom, and finally lashed out at his face
with a police whistle, giving him a black eye.

Jesse claimed to be so discomposed by the row that he
had no idea what happened next, until he suddenly found
himself with his hands around the throat of his aunt's dead
body. He left her on the bed in the back bedroom, and
wondered what to do throughout the following day. In the
evening he decided to dismember her for disposal and cut
off her legs, which he placed carefully on the table. Then
he lost his nerve, and fell to ruminating again.

The next day neighbours asked why Mrs Edmunds had

not appeared over the weekend, and were not satisfied by
Jesse's story that he had not seen her since Saturday's
noisy quarrel. A policeman was called, and arrested Jesse
as soon as he found the contents of the second-floor back
bedroom.

Jesse's confession might have reduced the charge to
manslaughter. Unfortunately it did not explain the
handkerchief stuffed into his aunt's mouth, presumably to
stop her from screaming. It had contributed to her suffocation, and supplied evidence of malice aforethought.

Joseph McKinstry, a Canadian soldier, was the last person
known to have seen prostitute Peggy Richards alive on the
night in 1942 before her body was found at the river's edge
beside **Waterloo Bridge**. She was bruised, and an attempt
had been made to throttle her.

McKinstry had turned her handbag over to the police
during the night, claiming he had met Peggy in a pub and
quarrelled with her, after which she had hit him with the
bag and run off leaving him holding it. Pressed by the
evidence of another witness he further admitted having
gone on the bridge with her and paid for services rendered.
But his story that she was alive when he left her could not
be disproved, and he was not convicted.

In 1950 a bus conductor named William Donoghue went
out for a little drink with his friend, driver Thomas Meaney.
A little drink consisted of as many pints as most hardened
boozers would consider a skinful, and about a bottle and a
half of spirits. After this heroic consumption, the two reeled
back to Mr Donoghue's flat in the gaunt thicket of **Peabody
Buildings** at the southern end of Duchy Street. There
they both collapsed into happy stupor, Mr Meaney in Mr
Donoghue's bed and Mr Donoghue on the sofa. After a

little, Mr Donoghue recovered consciousness, and recognized a pressing need to unload some of the beer, having done which he returned to his bed. Finding the recumbent Mr Meaney there, it occurred to Mr Donoghue's befuddled mind that his friend was always a practical joker. This object, Mr Donoghue decided, must be a tailor's dummy planted in his bed by way of a jest. He decided to get rid of it, and make sure it was never returned. With this in his alcohol-saturated mind, he stabbed Mr Meaney repeatedly with a kitchen-knife, threw him out of the apartment door on to the landing, and fell back to sleep the sleep of the just.

He awoke still squiffy rather than hungover, for neighbours discovered him next morning on the landing earnestly asking himself whether what lay before him was a body or a dummy. For if it was not a dummy, Mr Donoghue regretfully acknowledged, then he had killed a friend.

Understandably, the police found this extraordinary story unbelievable at first, and Mr Donoghue was committed for trial on a charge of murder. The Attorney-General disagreed, and Mr Donoghue was allowed to plead guilty to manslaughter.

The Borough High Street leads south through Newington Causeway to the great traffic junction of the Elephant and Castle. This acquired central prominence during the nineteenth century as the main coach and omnibus terminal for South London. To the southeast lie the crowded streets of Walworth; southwest, the more open roads of Kennington.

Travelling due west one eventually finds the Thames: a longitudinal reach carries it between Vauxhall and Charing Cross; it flows west-east again from Battersea to Vauxhall.

These two riverside districts were once famous for their
pleasure gardens.

Two distressing child murders are associated with the
Elephant and Castle. In 1908 Maria Ellen Bailes failed to
return from school in Islington. The following day her
body was found with its throat cut in a parcel in a men's
public lavatory on the corner of **St George's Road at the
Elephant.**

The murder ninety years earlier of Mary Albert in *Jacques
Court, Thomas Street* (which used to run **north of New Kent
Road, leading into Meadow Row**) was distinguished by
the absurdity of the murderer's motive. Robert Dean, a
clockmaker's assistant in 1818, wanted to marry a young
woman from Aldgate but her parents forbade the match.
Dean thought of killing himself in protest. Then, as the
emptiness of the romantic gesture dawned on him, he
determined to kill the young lady instead. Finally he
decided that the strongest protest he could make would be
to destroy an innocent child. So he lured Mary Albert into
the court with the promise of an apple, and cut her throat.

A later outburst of emotional bloodshed attracted large
crowds to gaze at the slum tenement of *4 Coraline Buildings*
in **West Square** (just south of St George's Road). Mary
Wetherley's husband was a street entertainer: he trundled
a performing seal around on a barrow, calling it his 'sea-
dog'. Mary succumbed briefly to the charms of a labourer
named William Heeley, and went to live with him. But
when she met Wetherley and the seal in the street, and
found her husband forgiving, she went back home to
Coraline Buildings.

Clearly Mary had a fatal fascination, for Heeley came
round as soon as he knew Wetherley and the seal were out
and cut her throat. He then barricaded himself in the

house and cut his own. The unhappy Wetherley tried to drown himself in a water-butt on hearing this dismal news. Happily for the seal he was rescued.

Samuel Quennell committed murder in consequence of a family quarrel that was not, for once, motivated by sexual passion. Quennell worked for his brother William, a Walworth builder. But he quarrelled with him, and told his fellow-labourer Daniel Fitzgerald that he would knock his brother's brains out. Fitzgerald, a habitual troublemaker, told William's wife what her brother-in-law had said: Mrs Quennell told her husband, and Samuel was given the fraternal sack.

He went out of his immediate neighbourhood to Lambeth New Cut and bought a pistol from a general dealer named Tubbs. Nearer home he bought shot from gunmaker John Mearns of 31 Walworth Road, and powder from William Welling, oilman, of 1 Amelia Street. This was just around the corner from Fitzgerald's lodgings in **Peacock Street**, and here Quennell lurked until his victim came home, whereupon he shot him dead.

Kennington's best-known murderer was a very twentieth-century figure: the resentful ex-husband paying alimony. Harry Dobkin's marriage had been arranged by an old-fashioned Jewish broker. He and Rachel Dubinski proved instantly incompatible, and separated after three days. But a son was conceived during that time, and Dobkin was compelled to pay maintenance for the next twenty years.

In fact, by 1940, the boy was fully grown and Rachel, a dependent whiner, believed that momentary matrimony entitled her to life-long support. Still, that did not entitle Dobkin to strangle her and bury her in the crypt of the Baptist church in **St Oswald's Place, close to 302 Kennington Lane**, where he was a fire-watcher.

A year later, when the bomb-damaged church was being cleared. Rachel's body was found. Her teeth were identified by her dentist, and Dobkin was unable to explain why he, the fire-watcher, had not given warning of the small fire in the chapel a year earlier which, it was now clear, had been intended to disguise the evidence of murder.

Dobkin made a fool of himself in the witness-box, clumsily trying to evade direct questions. He was convicted and hanged: had he been reprieved posterity might have allowed a little more sympathy for his unfortunate victim. As it is, few wives have been murdered to such a chorus of sympathy for their killers.

Auguste Dalmas lived in Battersea with his wife and four daughters until he was widowed in 1843. Then he slowly went to pieces, fell into debt, and retreated to lodgings in Brompton under an assumed name.

But Mrs Sarah Macfarlane, a widow of 13 Battersea Bridge Road, found the middle-aged Frenchman attractive and helped him find positions in domestic service for the girls. On April 29th the two took the youngest to a job in Chelsea. On their return, Dalmas was overcome by a fit of jealousy, and cut Mrs Macfarlane's throat on **Battersea Bridge**. She tottered into the *Swan and Magpie* on the Surrey side, where she died. He hid for a week, but was shown at his trial to have been demonstrably insane before the murder.

Prince of Wales Drive runs northeast from Battersea Bridge Road, skirting the south of Battersea Park. Off it ran *Clifton Gardens* in 1910, where an actor named Thomas Anderson (known on-stage as Atherstone) was mysteriously shot in the empty ground-floor flat at no 17.

Mr Anderson had lived for seven years in the flat above with a mistress, who was equally accepted by the sons of his marriage. One of them was dining with her on the night of the murder. Mr Anderson was not present, having absented himself for the night after a quarrel with the lady.

When two shots rang out, Anderson's son and mistress looked out of the window and saw a figure climbing over a neighbouring wall. When they hurried downstairs they found Anderson's body amid signs of a struggle in the empty flat. The clues were tantalizing: he was wearing carpet slippers, but his outdoor shoes were on the mantel-piece. His pocket contained a length of insulating cable, and his coat-tail held a cosh. The murder was never solved.

West of Battersea lies Wandsworth. The train murder of 1897 took place unnoticed here, for the bloodstained pestle which killed Elizabeth Camp was found on the line outside **Wandsworth Town station** (in the Putney direction). Miss Camp's body was discovered, pushed under a seat, when the evening train from Hounslow arrived in Waterloo. She was a barmaid with no known enemies, and had not been robbed or raped.

Although no charges were brought, senior police thought that the murder was committed by a heavily moustached man with what might have been bloodstains on his collar, who had two rums in the Alma near the station just after the train left. They believed he was identical with a demented clean-shaven vagrant who was committed shortly afterwards, and who was known to have bought and subsequently disposed of a false moustache. As they could not 'disguise' him in a moustache for an identity parade, they could not get a clear identification from witnesses.

12

—— Central South London ——

Clapham, Balham, Streatham, Peckham – 'homesteads' on arable land – expanded into villages whose proximity to London ultimately led to their development as continuous airy suburbs. Camberwell bore the air of an innocent converted village for so long that commentators apologized for the foul slum area surrounding Sultan Street until the beginning of the twentieth century. The apology often took the form of noting that the murderer Greenacre had lived here.

James Greenacre made a living by marrying, which gave him absolute title to his wives' fortunes. By Christmas 1836 he was preparing for his fourth wedding.

There were drawbacks. The most recent Mrs Greenacre was still alive, though in America. Still, he held her English real estate – slummy dwellings in the vicinity of Bowyer's Lane (today's Wyndham Road) and *Windmill Lane* (today's eastern end of **Bethwin Road**), lying between Camberwell Road and Camberwell New Road. Greenacre lived in one of the latter, *6 Carpenter's Place*. With him was Sarah Gale, the mother of his five-year-old daughter – 'Mrs Greenacre' in the eyes of the neighbours. But Sarah was more a co-conspirator than an obstacle.

Greenacre described himself as owning an estate in Hudson Bay. The lure attracted a washerwoman as calculating as himself: Hannah Brown, a connection of some

City acquaintance of Greenacre's, told him she had a nest-egg of over £300. The two agreed to marry at St Giles-in-the-Fields on Christmas Day and hold the reception at the home of their friends the Davises in Bartholomew Close in the City. Sarah made herself scarce, and on Christmas Eve Hannah went round for tea with her affianced. At eleven o'clock that night he appeared in Bartholomew Close bearing the news that the wedding was off: he had found Hannah using his name to gain credit at a tally-shop, and as she had no fortune he felt it would be unfair to make a pauper of her.

Neighbours saw Greenacre's shutters up on Christmas Eve, and they stayed up for nearly a week. Sarah Gale (Mrs Greenacre, as they believed) reappeared on Boxing Day.

On December 28th a passerby noticed a sack pushed behind a flagstone leaning against the wall of the newly built Cambridge Villas, near the Pineapple Toll-Gate in Edgware Road. Inspection revealed that it contained a woman's headless, limbless torso.

On January 6th 'Berkham Bob' Tomlin summoned the lock-keeper at Ben Jonson Lock on the Regent's Canal in Stepney. One of the gates was blocked and wouldn't open fully. The obstruction proved to be a woman's head.

On February 2nd a workman cutting osiers in Mr Tenpenny's field, south of Coldharbour Lane between Camberwell and Brixton (where the railway line now runs between Shakespeare Road and Hinton Road) found a pair of legs in a sack. The scattered parts were a perfect fit.

Tracing the sack from the potato merchant who had stamped his name on it to a builder who had owned it led to Greenacre. So did the complaints of Hannah's relatives who had not seen her since Christmas Eve.

The authorities, anxious to implicate Sarah, suggested that Greenacre had removed the remains in trunks which the local carrier took to the Elephant and Castle for him, about a week after Christmas. Although Greenacre, wishing to absolve Sarah, tried to telescope the removal of the body and omitted some details, his story is more likely. He probably spent Christmas Day cutting up the body and took the head, wrapped in a handkerchief on his knees, by omnibus from Camberwell to London and then by a second omnibus to Mile End, where he threw it over the parapet at the top of Canal Road. At 5.00 A.M. the next morning he took the legs down to the osier bed, returning for breakfast, after which he set out with the torso. It proved uncomfortably heavy, so he accepted a lift from a passing carter, slinging the sack on the tailboard and walking beside it to the Elephant and Castle. There he was unnerved by a passerby asking him what he'd got there, and made the rest of his journey to Paddington by cab.

He claimed that Hannah had tipped her chair over and killed herself by knocking her head against a block of wood on the floor. It was pointed out that someone had hit her with a stick-like object, putting her eye out. Greenacre then admitted that he had accidentally swung a silk-weaving roller which happened to hit her . . .

Before his execution he wrote sanctimoniously to his children, warning them to profit by his example and not to panic should they be present at fatal accidents. Such occurrences apparently ran in the family, for he reminded them of such misfortunes 'as that of your uncle, Samuel Greenacre, killing your Grandmother and shooting off your Aunt Mary's hand'.

A little to the east, a gang of amateurs perpetrated a murder of amazing savagery in 1980.

Brunswick Park is a seedy playground with tennis courts overlooked by a row of peeling grey houses on the south side. This once fine suburban terrace has largely turned to shabby bedsits. It was the given address of former boxer Donald Ryan, who was nearing fifty in the autumn of 1980 when he had the misfortune to meet young John Bowden and his companions.

These unpleasant drunks attacked lonely old people, as much for the fun of the violence as for the petty proceeds of robbery. David Begley, a porter from Winchcombe Street, Tooting, was the oldest of the group. Drink was slowly destroying him, but like Bowden (a labourer) he was still employed. Michael Ward, a 27-year-old gravedigger, was registered unemployed. He lived with Mrs Shirley Brindle in a comfortable little council maisonette in **Coleby Path**, a trim block running obliquely through the housing development **northeast of Brunswick Park**.

Ryan was invited back to Coleby Path where his hosts' murderous hospitality opened with a machete attack on him. He was then thrown into a scalding bath, and dismembered while still alive. A handsaw and an electric carving knife were used to detach his arms and legs. His head was put into the freezer after which the revelling murderers went out for another drink, scattering pieces of flesh on the waste ground and dustbins around the estate. They returned to sleep peacefully in the blood-slippery maisonette, and were utterly impenitent when arrested.

Mrs Brindle was not guilty of the murder, but received a suspended sentence for the relatively unimportant offence of preventing a burial. At the trial the jury required a recess, as the photographs of the offence made them physically sick. Ward continued to think the whole escapade had been a great joke. And as Bowden was hauled, struggling, to prison, he yelled at the judge, 'You old bastard! I hope you die screaming of cancer!'

The quiet suburb of Peckham has been remarkably free of infamous murderers, though Charley Peace (p. 217), who had previously lived in Lambeth and Greenwich, was an apparently placid, music-loving householder at 5 Evelina Road when his interrupted burglary in Blackheath led to his arrrest.

Brixton, to the west of Camberwell, has known its share of bloodshed. **Acre Lane** was quite a rustic retreat when William Jones lived in retirement at Springfield Cottage. At the age of eighty-four he was described as 'the kind old master' of Elizabeth Vickers. One wonders whether he had previously been her kind old keeper. For she was not the best of servants. She drank. When drunk she attacked Mr Jones. And as he grew infirm she beat him severely in these attacks. Ultimately he died from a beating. When it proved that he had bequeathed her £1000 this suggested malice aforethought, and Miss Vickers almost found herself written down a murderess rather than a manslaughterer.

One evening in 1923 a taxi-driver named Jacob Dickey drove from Victoria to Brixton, turned into Acre Lane, and again turned south into quiet suburban **Baytree Road**. The cab stopped at the top of the road and a man was seen wrestling with Dickey before three shots were fired, and Dickey was left dying.

The fugitive burst over the fence to the back gardens of Acre Lane (garage-yards have replaced the gardens now) and forced his way out to the main road through no 15. The main clue, found lying beside the body, was an unusual gold-topped walking stick incorporating a pencil-case. This was traced to a young criminal named James Vivian who cohabited with prostitute Hetty Colquhoun in Charlwood Street, Pimlico. Vivian claimed to have lent the stick to his friend Alexander 'Scottie' Mason, a story Mason at first corroborated.

The two young men and Miss Colquhoun seem to have concocted a joint story to exonerate them all. They suggested that the men intended to rob a house, and Mason had tried unsuccessfully to book a 'bent' taxi-driver at Victoria for their getaway. He thereafter made his own way to Brixton, when to his surprise the 'straight' driver Dickey turned up; a stranger emerged from the cab and a gun fired three times, causing Mason to make his undenied escape through Acre Lane. Vivian meanwhile swore that he had been unable to join Mason as he intended, having been confined to bed by a feverish cold.

The police disbelieved the entire farrago, and obviously thought that Mason or Vivian or both had engaged Dickey's taxi with intent to rob him. But since Mason had admitted possession of Vivian's stick and had confessed to being the one and only figure observed running away, while Hetty swore that Vivian had never left the house, it seemed hopeless to prosecute Vivian even when Mason changed his story to the accusation that Vivian had been the passenger in the cab. Still, the contradictions sufficed to gain Mason a reprieve. He was released from penal servitude in 1937 and died honourably in the Merchant Navy during the war.

Clapham sprawls. Bounded by Battersea to the north, Brixton to the east, Balham and Tooting to the south, and Wandsworth to the west, it is archetypal south London suburbia: reasonably open streets of terraced houses, often top-heavily ornamented with Victorian stucco over the doors, and some long, large shopping streets. For convenience, we may add the slightly upmarket districts of Stockwell and Balham at its northeast and southeast corners.

Late nineteenth-century Stockwell seems to imitate the St John's Wood *rus in urbis*. The streets are gracefully tree-lined; the houses definitely villas. Only a rather cramping absence of space indicates that the builders were less well-heeled than the developers of the North London paradise for kept women. The Rev. John Selby Watson fitted this respectable carefully budgeted neighbourhood. His home at *28* **St Martin's Road** has been replaced by modern flats, but the northern end of the road and the adjacent streets exemplify its kind. The Reverend John was headmaster of the Stockwell Grammar School. But in 1870 the governors dismissed him on grounds of age, and meanly refused him a pension.

The Reverend John had married a younger woman. By 1871 Ann Watson was upbraiding her husband for the penury they were both suffering and jeering at the impotence he now endured. This drove him to shoot her in a fit of rage, after which he shut himself up miserably in the house for two days, and tried unsuccessfully to poison himself.

Two of Stockwell's other claims to infamy are the presence in Grantham Road of Patrick Mackay (p. 99), who stayed there often with friends, and allowed their rather coarse teasing to drive him to his last murder in 1975; and the arrest at Mrs Smeed's boarding-house of Donald George Thomas (p. 182).

Lavender Hill runs across north Clapham: a broad road of shops and small businesses. Pretty Sophia Money lived at no 245 and worked for a local dairyman. On Sunday, 24th September 1905, she told a friend she was going for a walk. At a sweetshop she mentioned that she was off to Victoria. Thereafter she somehow got herself on to the 9.33 P.M. train from London Bridge to Brighton, and her body was thrown from it in the Merstham Tunnel, where it was found at 11.00 P.M. No explanation of her journey has ever been given. She was thought to have been seen furtively boarding the train at East Croydon and later struggling with a man in her compartment as the train passed through Purley Oaks. But her unexplained death added mystery to her life.

Sisters Avenue runs south off Lavender Hill, its rather large houses divided into flats. At 33a Frederick Browne lived with his wife, and was by all accounts a good husband. It is about the only praise anyone could find to bestow on this surly, violent man whose nearby garage at 7a Northcote Road, next to the Globe Cinema, was largely given over to stripping and reassembling stolen cars and bicycles.

His accomplice, William Kennedy, was an even more squalid criminal, with a string of convictions for petty pilfering and flashing.

In September 1927 the two travelled by rail to Billericay to burgle a house and steal a car. The burglary failed, but the car theft succeeded. As they drove through the night, PC Gutteridge flagged them down for a routine enquiry on the Ongar-Romford Road near Stapleford Abbots. When they could not give the number of the car, Browne panicked and shot the policeman. Then, with the callous touch that gave the crime lasting infamy, he shot out his victim's eyes. The two drove back to London and abandoned the car a couple of miles away from their home territory at the Camberwell Road end of Foxley Road.

It was some months before the police caught up with them. They were investigating another stolen car when a search of Browne's premises disclosed a pistol and cartridges which matched a spent cartridge the police had found in the abandoned murder vehicle. Browne and Kennedy were executed unlamented.

In the 1950s drape suits and teddy-boy clothes were teenage styles inviting challenge from other teenagers. On a summer evening in 1953 John Beckley and Matthew Chandler were walking past the bandstand on Clapham Common. Seeing some sharply dressed yobs approaching, the two hurled derisive insults at them. They may have been ready for a

fight, but they were unnerved by the shout of 'Get the
knives out!', and they took flight. The gang chased the pair
up to **Clapham Common North side** (the road which
borders the common for two-thirds of its length), where
the bus stops are all 'Request'. Beckley and Chandler
desperately flagged down a no 137, and Chandler boarded
it safely. Beckley was dragged off, and fell to a knife from
among the gang.

John Michael Davies was convicted of the murder. But
identification of a particular youth from a mob must always
be difficult; Davies was reprieved, and released after seven
years.

Clapham Common's most famous murder took place just
northwest of the bandstand. The path leading to Battersea
Rise passes some hummocky terrain on the left, which in
1900 still sported furze bushes. Leon Beron's battered body
was found here on New Year's morning, 1900. Steinie
Morrison (p. 43) was eventually convicted of the murder.
But the whole case belongs essentially to the immigrant
East End.

South of Battersea Rise runs **Almeric Road** where John
Reginald Christie (p. 134) was living in 1929 when he
attacked a woman with a cricket bat.

Elmhurst Mansions in **Elmhurst Road** lie **off Clapham
Manor Street**, which itself runs north off Clapham High
Street. In 1936 a middle-aged widow named Beatrice
Sutton was found strangled in her flat there. There was no
clue to her murder until a deserter from the RAF was
traced and arrested, whereupon he confessed to the killing.
Frederick Field (p. 61) tried to retract his confession in
court as he had already successfully done in the case of
Norah Upchurch. This time he failed to convince the judge
or jury of his innocence.

The further south one moves through Clapham the more salubrious and desirable the neighbourhood appears. Trinity Road runs from Tooting through Wandsworth Common, where Miss Elizabeth Ivatt ended her useful life (she had been a training college principal) in the comfortable mansion flats of **Chesham Court** close to the County Arms Hotel. In 1959 she was eighty-eight, but the companionship of Miss Phyllis Squires, more than twenty years younger, ensured that she was not lonely or helpless. There was no reason for the 35-year-old vagrant Ronald Benson to batter Miss Ivatt to death and try to burn her body. But then Benson was found quite unfit to plead, and I suppose one must see such a meaningless killing as a kind of natural disaster.

Far from natural was the notorious Balham Mystery of 1876. **The Priory, Bedford Hill** stands on the northern edge of **Tooting Bec Common**, a castellated ivory stucco fantasy. From the road its imposing front entrance suggests a mighty mansion. From the common, its simple construction as a pair of disguised boxes is more immediately apparent, as is the flat roof overlooked by bedroom windows whence traces of Charles Bravo's vomit were recovered with a silver spoon to be analysed for the presence of poison.

Florence Bravo and her husband were unlikeable members of the Victorian bourgeoisie. Florence was petty, selfish and dictatorial with her servants. Charles married her money rather than Florence herself, and was quite prepared to break off the engagement if she quibbled about making him sole legal possessor of all she owned. Florence came to terms because she wanted respectability as well as prosperity; once that was achieved she sulked over Charles's parsimony with 'her' wealth.

Young Florence Campbell had earlier been rushed into

an unhappy but socially acceptable marriage. Captain Alexander Ricardo was rich and well-connected, and the Campbells encouraged their nineteen-year-old daughter's wedding. They did not know that the groom was a brutal alcoholic, and they offered their unhappy daughter no help when she made this discovery. Florence's wish for a separation was overruled and the young couple were packed off to Malvern for a 'water cure' at the hydropathic establishment of Dr James Manby Gully.

Here Florence found a sympathetic friend. Dr Gully helped her arrange a separation. The Campbells were furious, and Florence's father cut off her allowance. But Ricardo solved her financial problem by dying of a last drinking bout. Since their separation was not complete, Florence inherited his considerable fortune and enjoyed full financial independence. (Nobody at the time, or for many years after Florence's death, saw any significance in the discovery of a small quantity of tartar emetic in Alexander Ricardo's body.)

Had Dr Gully been able to marry Florence, she might have remained unknown to history. Unfortunately he already possessed a wife, and though the couple had been estranged for many years and Mrs Gully was almost twenty years older than he, the lady obstinately refused to die. Florence became the companion and lover of this generous, well-informed older man. To her parents' fury the couple travelled on the continent together, and although the outward proprieties were respected Florence once suffered a miscarriage that may have been induced by Dr Gully.

Like Adelaide Bartlett (p. 75), Florence found the strain of fecundity an intolerable addition to the burden of sex. Abruptly she withdrew her favours from the doctor, took as a female companion the sallow, frumpish bespectacled widow Jane Cox, and returned to England where she

–

leased The Priory. Gully accepted the dismissal, but took a house nearby to continue social friendship.

Despite her command of a fifteen-room house with a staff of twelve, the companionship of Mrs Cox and the admiration of Dr Gully, Florence wanted more. She wanted to be accepted as a lady. This meant reconciliation with her parents – which meant marriage.

Mrs Cox suggested just the suitor. Young lawyer Charles Bravo had no special wish to continue living under his parents' comfortable roof at 2 Palace Green, Kensington. He would be willing to become master of The Priory, even if that also meant becoming the husband of Florence Ricardo. And so the young couple entered into convenient wedlock in December 1875.

Their marriage did not last long. In April 1876 Charles came home badly shaken by a ride in which his horse had bolted. Florence also claimed to be feeling unwell, did not drink her normal glass of burgundy at dinner, and went to bed soon after they had eaten. Charles retired half an hour later. Suddenly he appeared on the landing in his nightshirt bawling for Florence and hot water. Mrs Cox duly brought the water, and urged Charles to swallow a mustard emetic while she prepared a mustard footbath. Florence had to be aroused to join her husband, who was clearly seriously ill.

A host of doctors attended the dying man over the next two days, including the celebrated Sir William Gull (who has long been a popular, if thoroughly unlikely, candidate for 'Jack the Ripper'). All agreed that Charles had swallowed an irritant poison but that no help could be offered if he did not identify it. The patient obstinately insisted that he had done no more than rub laudanum on his gums as a treatment for neuralgia.

After his death a post-mortem established that he had ingested a massive dose of tartar emetic.

The local coroner tried to suppress all scandal. He

rushed through a furtive inquest, and urged the jury to accept Mrs Cox's story that Charles had confessed to taking poison. The jury refused and returned an open verdict. The attorney-general was forced to notice the public outcry and order a second inquest.

This time Mrs Cox subtly changed her story. She permitted the history of Florence's liaison with Dr Gully to be extracted from her, which skilfully distracted attention from the possibility that Florence was a murderess who could have put poison in the burgundy or in the carafe of drinking-water from which Charles habitually took a hearty swig before getting into bed. The public was excited by the revelation that she was a fornicatress. There was now a reason for Charles's having (in the words Jane Cox ascribed to him) 'taken poison for Dr Gully'.

The jury was still not satisfied. But they could not pin the administration of poison either on to Gully (who had the drug in his pharmocopeia, but not the opportunity) or Florence (who had the opportunity but not, as far as they knew, the drug). Nor did they suggest a conspiracy between the two. They affirmed their belief that Charles had been wilfully murdered, but regretted that 'there is not sufficient proof to affix the guilt upon any person or persons'.

But Florence *did* have access to tartar emetic: it was used in her stables, as she knew. The poison was probably administered through the water carafe: Charles's sudden demand for hot water suggests an immediate reaction to the thirty-grain dose.

Florence drank herself to death in a few years. Dr Gully was socially ruined. The mystery remains. But we cannot overlook that both the young widow's husbands had at one time or another consumed tartar emetic.

13

—————— Southeast London ——————

Southeast London contains dockland and naval institutions on the river at Greenwich and Deptford; the open spaces of Greenwich Park, Blackheath and Eltham Common farther south; the rougher area of Deptford, whose slums once compared with the worst of Whitechapel and St Giles; and Blackheath with its airy and luxurious villas. There are also the areas of Lewisham and Catford, which proffer restrained lower-middle-class suburbia.

Edmund Pook's story carries us from north to south of the district. In 1871 his family lived at 3 London Road, Greenwich (now the completely redeveloped end of Greenwich High Road), and employed 17-year-old Jane Clouson as a maid. Jane lived at 12 Ashburnham Road (now Place) nearby, in a neat terraced cottage which is today the only pebble-dashed house in the street.

Edmund was twenty and, as masters and maids did, the two became friendlier than Mrs Pook could approve. She sacked the girl, but Jane, by now pregnant, believed Edmund would make an honest woman of her and told a friend she was going to meet him.

The next time anyone saw Jane she was crawling along *Kidbrooke Lane* (today's **Brook Lane**) **on the edge of Eltham Common**. She was sobbing; her head was battered, and one eye hung from its socket. She died in Guy's Hospital.

Edmund had been seen running away from Kidbrooke

Lane. Mud and blood were found on his trousers. And a shopkeeper had sold him a hammer that appeared to be the murder weapon. Still, his claim to have spent the whole night outside another girlfriend's house in Lewisham could not be disproved. He was acquitted, and an outraged crowd demonstrated against the Pook family in Greenwich.

Another young man's brutal sex-crime took place on **Eltham Common** in 1918. 21-year-old David Greenwood raped and strangled 16-year-old Nellie Trew on the common **beside Well Hall Road**. He lost his army regimental badge in the struggle, and also an overcoat button which had been fastened with wire rather than sewn with cotton. These were recognized by his workmates at Hewson's Manufacturing of Newman Street (running north off Oxford Street). Greenwood was sentenced to life imprisonment, not death, as his war record was good and there was also some doubt as to whether he was really strong enough to have killed Nellie.

Martha Brixey, a Greenwich under-nursemaid, worked for Mrs Ffinch whose husband was a solicitor in *London Road* in 1842. When the servants were given black dresses to mourn a death in the family, Martha constantly tore hers, which was uncomfortable. While Mrs Ffinch was away she 'wished it at the devil' and burned it, an offence which Sarah May the upper-nursemaid priggishly 'thought it her duty to inform her mistress' on Mrs Ffinch's return.

Martha was given notice, to which she responded by suffocating the baby and then hysterically telling the household and asking them whether Mr Ffinch might forgive her in a week's time. She was found guilty but insane.

The **Greenwich Naval Hospital** was a sanctuary for retired sailors as Chelsea was for soldiers. In 1833 James

Ward was in the Physicians' Ward with high fever and a racking cough. Demented by his fever, the old boy concluded that another pensioner, named Bailey, was laughing at his distress and killed him with his clasp-knife. Ward's responses to questioning were so disordered that no one ever imagined him fit to plead.

In 1905 Mr and Mrs Thomas Farrow managed Mr Chapman's chandler's shop at **34 Deptford High Street**. A pair of burglar brothers lived nearby: Albert Stratton at 67 Knott Street (today's Creekside, between Creek Road and Deptford Church Street), and Alfred at Brookmill Road, on the other side of Deptford Bridge.

The Strattons robbed the shop – battering the Farrows to death when they were disturbed. Inadequate recognition and identification of them as the two men seen running from the premises (they wore stocking masks) was fully compensated by Alfred's thumbprint which was left on a cashbox. This was the first murder case in England to be settled in court by expert testimony on a fingerprint.

Further east, in Plumstead, 37-year-old widow Louisa Jane Taylor went to live with an old couple called Tregillis in *3 Naylor's Cottages* (now destroyed). She flirted with Mr Tregillis, and lovingly nursed his wife through a long, deteriorating illness which started shortly after Louisa's arrival. She puzzled 90-year-old Tregillis by suggesting that they exchange wills in each other's favour, and aroused his suspicion when he realized that she had purloined his pension. Their doctor was alerted but diagnosed too late that Mrs Tregillis was dying from the sugar of lead Lousia had been administering.

St John's Park is a road of massive Victorian villas off the northeastern edge of Blackheath. On a quiet night in 1878 a policeman saw a light moving in the back of no 2. When he went to investigate, a man fired a pistol at him and scrambled away toward the garden, where he was caught. The cat-burglar Charley Peace, who had been preying on south London for several years, had been apprehended at last.

But Peace was also a murderer. He had killed Arthur Cross outside his home in Banner Street, Sheffield, after harrassing him for some time with his sadistic pursuit of Mrs Cross. Flight from this murder had brought him south to Greenwich, Lambeth and finally Peckham, where he lived as Mr Johnson, enjoying musical evenings at which he performed on some of the many violins he had stolen.

After his conviction he further admitted to the killing of a policeman in Manchester: a crime for which two brothers were languishing in prison. His pathological violence, coarse self-indulgence and occasional sanctimoniousness made him a quite loathsome villain, in spite of which he achieved some popular esteem as a kind of irrepressible rogue.

Greenwich High Street runs south to Lewisham Road and Lewisham High Street which in turn continues to Rushey Green Road, Catford. In this down-to-earth suburban territory some professional criminals of South London fought out their differences in 1966. *'Mister Smith and the Witch Doctor'* was the resounding name of a drinking club in **Rushey Green Road**. Here the Richardson mob turned up on March 8th to enforce their domination over local organized crime. In the mêlée Frankie Fraser, Eddie Richardson and two others were injured, and Richard Charles Hart was shot dead. No one was convicted of his murder, though several men were charged with 'causing an affray'. But the affair caused bad blood among the London mobs, and their division contributed to the death

of 'Ginger' Marks (p. 41) and the excesses of the Richardsons and Krays (p. 40) which ultimately enabled the police
to break up the gangs.

Parallel to Rushey Green Road, three blocks to the west,
runs **Doggett Road**. Maxwell Confait, a transvestite homosexual prostitute, had a bed-sittingroom in no 27, in which
he was found strangled when the house caught fire in the
middle of the night in April 1974. Police extracted confessions from three youths, the oldest of whom was mentally
subnormal, and they were convicted of murder, manslaughter and arson.

A year later, Christopher Price MP forced a reconsider-
ation of their case, as it seemed Confait had died before the
fire started and not as stated in their confessions. Although
the Court of Appeal quashed the convictions, a Home
Office enquiry seemed to aim mainly at whitewashing the
police. Five years later it was definitely established that
Confait had died several hours before the fire started, and
two men in prison were said to have admitted their
responsibility. Compensation was at last paid to the boys
in 1981, and the authorities' attempts to justify their
handling of the case seem pretty unconvincing.

Penge, southwest of Catford on the edge of Crystal
Palace Park, was a dormitory village on the outskirts of
South London in 1877 when four young people shepherded
an invalid into lodgings at *34 Forbes Road* (now **Mosslea
Road**, running **north off the High Street**) with a view to
taking her on to the London Hospital for treatment. Harriet
Staunton died before she could be removed, and the local
doctor treating her was shocked by her total emaciation
and filthy condition. It was strange that she should have
died of starvation and neglect since one of the well-
nourished young people accompanying her was her
husband.

Louis Staunton, self-described as an auctioneer, had married the older, educationally subnormal Harriet in 1875 and taken her to live in a bijou semi at 8 Loughborough Park Road, Brixton. (A very attractive road, then, offering an 1870s equivalent of starting marriage in a new Wimpey house.) A baby was born to them the following year, and then Louis moved to 6 Colby Road, Gipsy Hill, while his brother and sister-in-law, Patrick and Elizabeth Staunton, who had been living almost opposite them at 29 Loughborough Park Road, went down to Firth Cottage at Cudham in Kent.

Soon Harriet and the baby were sent to join them in Cudham, and Louis paid Patrick £1 a week for their keep while he enjoyed the embraces of Elizabeth's sister, Alice Rhodes, at Gipsy Hill. Patrick, an unsuccessful artist, probably needed the money. Louis, whatever his income from the auctioneering, was comfortably off since Harriet had brought a nest-egg of £3000 to the marriage.

All the Stauntons (and Alice Rhodes) found Harriet an encumbrance. But Patrick was cruel and violent in addition. He and Elizabeth kept Harriet and the baby confined to one room, refused to let visitors see them, and literally starved the poor woman to death. Louis and Alice came down to Cudham and stayed at Little Gray's Farm, content that Harriet should remain in Patrick's care while Alice was pregnant.

Early in April 1877 the baby became so seriously ill that the Stauntons raced it to the London Hospital. It died there, and the cruel young people suddenly realized that Harriet's condition was equally dangerous. Within a week they had made the arrangements to move her to Penge, but they were too late. When Harriet's mother, who had been denied contact with her daughter, heard of the girl's condition at the time of her death proceedings against the Stauntons were started.

They were very unpopular defendants and the judge was undeniably biased against them. He savaged Alice Rhodes for her immorality, understressed Louis' defence that the weekly payment of £1 was adequate care for his wife, and overrode the medical experts who asserted that Harriet's demise might easily be the result of meningitis rather than starvation.

The last point carried the day after the four had been sentenced to death. Alice and Elizabeth were granted free pardons, and the men had their sentences commuted to life imprisonment.

Seventy-five years later, Derek Bentley and Chris Craig were living west of Penge in the modern suburb of Norbury. Both lived just off the London Road: Bentley at 1 Fairview Road, near Norbury station, and Craig a few blocks south at 9 Norbury Court Road. They were in their teens, and adopted drape suits and trilby hats to give themselves a gangster-film image.

Early in 1952 they went out together in the evening, took a bus to Croydon and climbed on to Barlow and Parker's warehouse in **Tamworth Road**, hoping to break in and find something worth stealing. No sooner were they on the roof than the police arrived: the boys had been spotted climbing over the yard gate by a neighbour.

There followed half an hour of havoc. The first policeman on the roof approached them and collared Bentley. Craig, who always carried a gun, responded to Bentley's alleged cry of, 'Let him have it, Chris!' by firing and wounding the officer, and kept up intermittent firing across the roof as long as his ammunition held out. In the course of this gunplay Constable Miles was shot dead as he leaped from the staircase head on to the roof. Bentley was taken away to a police car, reproaching Craig for the murder. When his bullets were spent Craig flung himself off the roof, suffering severe injuries.

Juvenile delinquency turned lethal was a matter of serious concern to the authorities. Lord Chief Justice Goddard saw to it that the boys were given a tense and hostile trial. When both were convicted, Bentley was sentenced to death, but Craig was too young for any sentence but indeterminate imprisonment.

It was obviously unjust to hang a boy for being the 18-year-old accomplice of a 16-year-old who had actually fired the gun, especially when it was unlikely that Bentley had expected Craig to use it and had been under arrest at the time of the killing. But the powers-that-be were determined to make an exhibition of somebody. In so doing they exposed the vindictiveness of their 'retributive justice', made a martyr of Derek Bentley, and contributed very substantially to the abolition of capital punishment.

14

—————— **Southwest London** ——————

The lush suburbs of the southwest, hosting the Boat
Race and the All England Tennis Championship, seem to
continue the genteel enthusiasms and decorous creature
comfort of Edwardian life. Moving away from the river
and Putney centre, roads become broader and quieter:
gardens larger and richer. Yet murders have occurred in
this tranquil region.

In 1842 Putney Heath extended from Putney Hill to
Roehampton. One of the few large houses on the open
space was *Granard Lodge*, whose main gate and gatehouse
still stand on **Putney Park Lane** (itself a surviving unme-
talled private road **running from Upper Richmond
Road to Putney Heath Road**).

In April 1842 the Granard Lodge coachman was a dark
thinning-haired Irishman of 50 named Daniel Good.

It was a fine evening when Good drove his master's
four-wheeler along Wandsworth High Street and stopped
at Mr Collingbourne's shop for a pair of breeches, which
Mr Collingbourne was happy to let him take on credit. As
he left the shop, Good quietly purloined a pair of trousers.

Samuel Dagnell, Collingbourne's assistant, spotted the
theft and called his master. PC William Gardner,
accompanied by Dagnell (to identify Good) and another
boy named Speed (to identify Granard Lodge) toiled across
the heath in the dark to the Lodge, where he insisted on
looking for the missing trousers.

Good's objections to a search were overruled by head gardener Thomas Oughton, who joined the searchers together with Good's 11-year-old son, another Daniel. Two of the four stables were searched without incident. At the third Good demurred, and started shifting bundles of hay in one of the stalls. Gardner ordered him to stop, set the two boys to watch him, and went to see what Good was hiding.

'Why, what is this? Here's a goose!' said the policeman on uncovering Good's hiding-place. Instantly Good rushed out of the building, locking the stable door behind him. Gardner left Speed to try and force the lock with a pitchfork, and went back to examine the goose.

'It's not a goose; it's a sheep', he remarked as he pulled it out. Dagnell ventured that it might be a human being, and it dawned on them all that they were in fact looking at a woman's disembowelled torso. They rushed at the locked door and escaped into the yard by main force.

Good had disappeared in the direction of London, and was not to be captured for ten days, during which time it was established that the body was that of his pregnant common-law wife Jane Good, alias Jones, alias Sparks. She was the third woman with whom Good had enjoyed an apparently permanent liaison and he intended to make a further change and 'marry' 16-year-old Susan Butcher, a carpenter's daughter from Woolwich. Susan had been given some of Jane's clothes but was quite ignorant that their owner was dead.

Good himself, after escaping from the stable, hid for a day with his first wife, a forceful Irishwoman called Molly who sold fruit in Bishopsgate and lodged at Flower and Dean Street, Whitechapel. Then he moved on for two more days with a nephew in Deptford, who had not previously known of his existence. Then, disguised in a new suit of fustians, he made his way to Tonbridge and took work as a bricklayer's mate on a building site. It was his misfortune to be recognized by an ex-policeman from Putney, and arrested.

Nobody knew how Jane had actually been killed before she was dismembered. Most of her body had been burned on a massive fire in the harness-room grate at Granard Lodge. Good offered the feeble explanation that she had cut her own throat from jealousy of Susan and that an unknown matchseller from Brompton, who had offered to dispose of the body for a guinea, had accomplished the fearful dismembering and burning. His crime shocked the country more than any since Greenacre's (p. 202). But his love-life made an almost equal impression. Lord Denman in sentencing him rebuked his 'indulgence of your inclinations for one woman after another'.

Putney Heath converges with Richmond Park and Wimbledon Common at the junction of Roehampton Lane with Kingston Road. Windmill Road tracks from the junction across the northern corner of Wimbledon Common (or Putney Vale), and a bridle path diverges from it to lead eastward to Wimbledon Park Side. Noisy and busy traffic highways deface the edges of this South London grassland, and the **Queensmere Tunnel** is a necessary adjunct for pedestrians wishing to escape from suburbia to parkland and back. In the 1960s it was also a trysting place for all-male lovers, which earned it the nickname 'Queersmere'. One summer evening in 1969 a gang of youths from Alton Estate, west of Putney Vale, wandered on to the common 'queer-bashing'.

Michael de Gruchy, a solicitor's clerk, was crossing the common as the yobs approached. Someone shouted 'Charge!' and the gang chased and overtook de Gruchy, whom they killed. Eventually ten boys were convicted of various crimes connected with the killing. Of the three convicted of murder only Geoffrey Hammond was old enough to have his name publicized.

South of Queensmere and a little to the east lies the All England Lawn Tennis Club. **Somerset Road** backs this and became the peaceful setting for a most unlikely confrontation in 1938. 'Irish Rose' Atkins, a 30-year-old prostitute, encountered a van driver called George Brain who lived with his parents nearby. He was the sole survivor of the meeting, and his account was that after offering him her professional services she attempted to blackmail him. This distressed him so much that he 'blacked out', and had no recollection what happened next, though he could not deny that his subsequent actions included stealing £32 from his employers (a wholesale bootmakers in St Pancras) and absconding to the Isle of Sheppey.

When the police found him, nine days later, they filled in the significant details: Miss Atkins had been stabbed, had been beaten over the head with a starting handle and had been run over by Brain's van as she lay in the road. They felt that Mr Brain had been unduly thorough in eliminating his victim, and they surmised that his motive was robbery. They speculated that the discovery that Miss Atkins was only carrying 4 shillings (20p) had prompted the more successful robbery of Brain's employers. The jury agreed with the police.

Due east of the Lawn Tennis shrine and over a golf course lies long, winding, hilly, Arthur Road. Much of it is lined with large desirable detached houses, and it was here that the Hosein Brothers (p. 178) trailed the *News of the World's* directorial Rolls Royce in December 1969. The incompetent kidnappers believed they were discovering the home of the newspaper's proprietor, Mr Rupert Murdoch. But 20 Arthur Road was the home of the company's deputy

chairman, Mr Alec McKay, and anyone but the Hoseins
would have thought Mr Murdoch a modest multi-million-
aire indeed to content himself with a house so close to a
main road, comfortable and attractive though it is. It is
surprising, too, to imagine the pair carrying out the violent
abduction of Mrs McKay with so little screening from any
passer-by.

Half a mile to the south, Worple Road and Alexandra
Road converge with Wimbledon Hill and The Broadway
to form the centre of Wimbledon. Small boys in blazers of
hideous hues abound, indicating the presence of a number
of private schools in the surrounding area. Such schools
existed as early as 1881, among them Mr Bedbrook's
Blenheim House at *1 and 2* **St George's Road**. Young
Percy John was one of Mr Bedbrook's pupils. On December
3rd he received a fraternal visit from his brother-in-law, a
physician named George Henry Lamson. For the boy's
delectation, Lamson had brought a fruitcake, which was
sliced and eaten in the headmaster's parlour. He also gave
him a capsule full of sugar. Shortly afterwards the lad died
with symptoms of poisoning. The capsule had evidently
been intended to divert attention from the cake, into one
slice of which, and one only, Lamson had injected aconite.
He had succeeded in forcing this slice on Percy.

   Lamson was financially pressed, and would have welcomed having his wife's patrimony increased by the
addition of her brother's share. He was one of several
poisoning doctors in Victorian Britain, but the only one to
be convicted and hanged for a crime committed in London.
St George's Road runs southwest from the town centre.
Although its inner end now comprises large shop and office
blocks, its outer extremity still holds the type of comfortable
semi-detached houses which conveniently converted to
small private schools in the late nineteenth century.

The Ridgway and Copse Hill lead westward from Wimbledon in the direction of the Kingston by-pass and Richmond Park. **Lindisfarne Road** is a charming cul-de-sac leading **south off Copse Hill**, comprising decent-sized,, detached brick houses, many with leaded windows. The gardens are well-tended and beautifully stocked.

In 1938 Percy Casserley lived at **no 35**. He was an elderly alcoholic, whose sullen drunkenness and consequent impotence severely damaged his marriage. Mrs Ena Casserley started an affair with a handsome young builder's foreman who worked nearby, and before long was carrying a child for him. She sought a divorce from Percy but he refused.

When serious marital strife threatened, Ted Chaplin came round to the house to try and persuade Percy to end the unhappy marriage. Percy was annoyed to learn that Chaplin was the father of his wife's forthcoming child. A quarrel ensued, and a loaded pistol Percy kept in his drawer was produced. When the quarrel ended, Mr Casserley lay shot dead on the floor.

Mr Chaplin's explanation to the police was a familiar story: Percy had produced the pistol, and it had gone off accidentally in the struggle. It was not helpful to this tale that Percy had been coshed before he was shot, and Ted admitted taking the cosh with him in case of trouble.

But the story has a happy ending. The jury accepted an element of accident, and Mr Chaplin was sentenced to twelve years for manslaughter. On his release, Mrs Casserley met him and they were married at last.

The homicide house, no 35, stands out starkly in the warm close. It has been whitewashed and its garden paved over.

Appendix

– Topography of London Murder –

Obsolete place and building names in **_bold italic._**
Murderers in **bold**
Victims in _italic_

171 *Globe Lane,* **Robert Emmett**
172 Bow Road, **John Stockwell**
173 Evering Road, **Reginald Kray**
174 *Nova Scotia Gardens,* **Bishop & Head**
175 Park Road, **Cyril Maltby**
176 Carlton Vale *Tommy Smithson*
177 Westpoint Trading Estate, **'Jack the Stripper'**
178 Great West Road, **Hulten & Jones**
179 Park Road, **Kate Webster**
180 Braybrook Road, **Roberts, Witney & Duddy**
181 *Linden House,* **Thomas Wainewright**
182 Winscombe Crescent, **Linford Derrick**
183 Montpelier Avenue, **Ronald Chesney**
184 Charteris Road, **Michael Dowdall**
185 *Ladysmith Avenue,* **George Crossman**
186 Mayo Road, **Amelia Dyer**
187 *Muswell Lodge,* **Millsom & Fowler**
188 Finchley Road, **Donald Hume**
189 North Circular Road, **Grahame Young**
190 Melrose Avenue, **Dennis Nilson** *(12 victims)*
191 Cranley Gardens, **Dennis Nilsen** *(3 victims)*
192 *Grove Place,* **William Allnutt**

193 Railway between Bow and Hackney Wick, **Franz Müller**
194 Bethune Road, **Louise Masset**
195 Scotland Green, **George Woolf**
196 Mitchley Road, **Hefeld & Jacob**
197 Wades Hill, **Donald Thomas**
198 Bartholomew Square, **George Chapman** *(Mary Spink)*
199 *Kidbrooke Lane,* **Edmund Pook**
200 Well Hall Road, **David Greenwood**
201 *London Road,* **Martha Brixey**
202 Deptford High Street, **Albert & Alfred Stratton**
203 *Naylors Cottages,* **Louisa Taylor**
204 Rushey Green Road, *Richard Hart*
205 Doggett Road, *Maxwell Confait*
206 *Forbes Road,* **The Stauntons**
207 Putney Park Lane, **Daniel Good**
208 Queensmere Subway, *Michael de Gruchy*
209 Somerset Road, **George Brain**
210 St George's Road, **Dr Lamson**
211 Lindisfarne Road, *Percy Casserley*
212 Ashwin Street, **Thomas Orrock**

MAP A

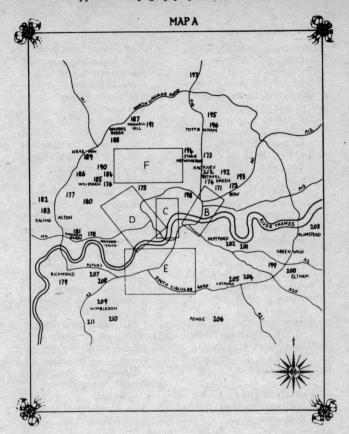

KEY TO MAP B
CITY AND EAST END

1 Tower of London, *The Little Princes* and *Sir Thomas Overbury*
2 Bunhill Fields, **John Price**
3 East Cheap, **Robert Blakeley**
4 Post Office Court, **Kitty Byron**
5 Fenchurch Street Station, **Edward Hopwood**
6 Exchange Buildings, **George Gardstein's gang**
7 Birchin Lane, **Jenkins & Hedley**
8 *Church Street,* **Thomas Corrigan**
9 Goodman's Yard, **Eliza Ross** and **Enoch Mobbs** **Jack the Ripper**
10 Brick Lane, *Emma Smith*
11 *George Yard,* *Martha Tabram*
12 *Bucks Row,* *Polly Nicholls*
13 Hanbury Street, *Annie Chapman*
14 *Berner Street,* *Elizabeth Stride*
15 Mitre Square *Catherine Eddowes*
16 *Dorset Street,* *Mary Kelly*
17 *Castle Alley,* *Alice McKenzie*
18 *Swallow Gardens,* *Frances Coles*
19 *Ratcliffe Highway,* **John Williams** *(the Marrs)*, **John Pegsworth**

20 *New Gravel Lane,* **John Williams** *(the Williamsons)*
21 *Rupert Street,* **Morris & Marks Reubens**
22 Vine Court, **Henry Wainwright**
23 Turner Street, **William Seaman**
24 Philpot Street, **Oreman, McCoy & Brozhevishsky**
25 *Grove Street,* **Mark Godmacher**
26 Whitechapel Road, **Ronald Kray**
27 Cheshire Street, *Ginger Marks*
28 *Greenbank,* **Edward Dwyer**
29 *Minerva Place,* **The Mannings**
30 *Higglers Lane,* *Elizabeth Winterflood*
31 Union Street, **George Chapman** *(Bessie Taylor)*
32 Borough High Street, **George Chapman** *(Maud Marsh)*
33 St George's Road, *Marie Bailes*
34 *Jacques Court,* **Robert Dean**
35 West Square, **William Heeley**
36 Peacock Street, **Samuel Quennell**
37 Batty Street, **Israel Lipski**

MAP B

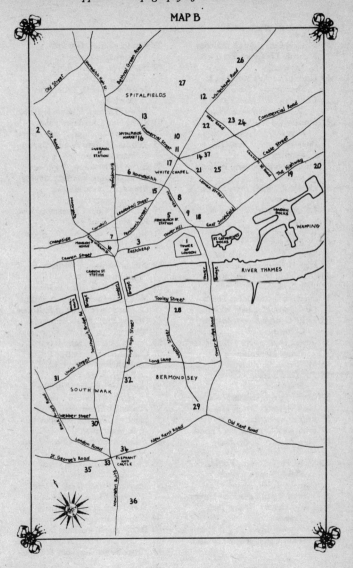

RIVER THAMES

KEY TO MAP C

AROUND THE WEST END

38 Tanfield Court, **Sarah Malcom**
39 *Fleur de Lis Court,* **Elizabeth Brownrigg**
40 *Gray's Inn Fields,* **Evans & Sherwood** *(Thomas Claxton)*
41 *Clerkenwell Fields,* **Evans & Sherwood** *(Rowland Holt)*
42 *Hockley-in-the-Hole,* **Evans & Sherwood** *(Michael Low)*
43 Chancery Lane, **Elizabeth Fenning**
44 Mecklenbergh Square, **William Sapwell**
45 *Coldbath Fields Prison,* **George Hewson**
46 *Coldbath Fields Prison,* **Michael Barrett**
47 Wilmington Square, **Charles Ellsome**
48 Safffron Hill, **Mogni & Pelizzioni**
49 High Holborn, *Dorothy Wallis*
50 Gray's Inn Road, **Socrates Petrides**
51 Short's Gardens, **John Thrift**
52 *Coal Yard,* **Matthew Welch**
53 *Little George Street,* **Joseph Connor**
54 Covent Garden Opera House, **Rev. James Hackman**
55 Maiden Lane, **Richard Prince**
56 *Portland Street,* **William Bousfield**
57 *Broad Street,* **Michael Stöltzer**
58 Little Newport Street, *Max Kassell*
59 Rupert Street, *Rita Barrett*
60 Broadwick Street, *Rachel Fenwick*
61 Long Acre, *Helen Freedman*
62 Goslett Yard, *Freddie Mills*
63 Shaftesbury Avenue, **Frederick Field** *(Norah Upchurch)*
64 Carnaby Street, *Margaret Cook*
65 Tyburn Road, **Catherine Hayes**
66 *Lyons Corner House,* **Jack Tratsart**
67 Glasshouse Street, *Marius Martin*
68 Denman Street, **Jeannie Baxter**

69 Wardour Street, **Gordon Cummins** *(Evelyn Oatey)*
70 Gosfield Street, **Gordon Cummins** *(Margaret Lowe)*
71 *Leicester Fields,* **Theodore Gardelle**
72 *Howard Street,* **Mohun & Hill**
73 Savoy Hotel, **Madame Fahmy**
74 House of Commons, *Spencer Perceval*
75 *Salopian Coffee House,* **Daniel Macnaughton**
76 House of Commons, *Airey Neave*
77 Birdcage Walk, **Annette Mayers**
78 *Brewers Green,* **Martha Browning**
79 Pall Mall, **Count Königsmark**
80 Pall Mall, **Lord Byron**
81 St James's Square, *Yvonne Fletcher*
82 Claverton Street, **Adelaide Bartlett**
83 Tachbrook Street, **William Holmyard**
84 Rochester Row, **John Robinson**
85 Montague Place, **William Jeffe**
86 Charlotte Street, **Voisin & Roche**
87 Grafton Way, **Marie Hermann**
88 Whitfield Street, *Doris Piernecke*
89 Bruton Street, **Sarah Metyard**
90 Chester Square, **Arthur Boyce**
91 Lower Belgrave Street, **Lord Lucan**
92 Hungerford Bridge, **Patrick Mackay** *(unknown tramp)*
93 *Frederick Street,* **Eliza Davis**
94 Lambeth Bridge, **Grondkowski & Malinowski** *(Frank Everitt)*
95 *Duke Street,* **Neill Cream** *(Ellen Donworth)*
96 Lambeth Road, **Neill Cream** *(Matilda Clover)*
97 Stamford Street, **Neill Cream** *(Emma Shrivell & Alice Marsh)*
98 York Road, **Frederick Jesse**
99 Waterloo Bridge, *Peggy Richards*
100 Duchy Street, **William Donoghue**
101 St Oswald's Place, **Harry Dobkin**
102 *Cross Street,* **Maycock & Pope**

MAP C

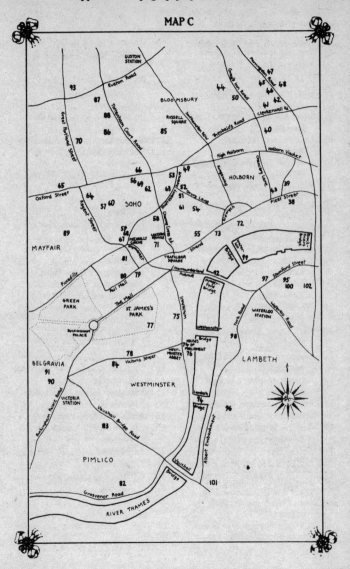

KEY TO MAP D
KENSINGTON AND CHELSEA

82 Claverton Street, **Adelaide Bartlett**

83 Tachbrook Street, **William Holmyard**

90 Chester Square, **Arthur Boyce**

91 Lower Belgrave Street, **Lord Lucan**

104 Cato Street, **Arthur Thistlewood**

105 Portman Square, **Robinson & the Craigs**

106 *Spencer Hotel,* **Henry Jacoby**

107 Montagu Place, **Gordon Cummins** *(Evelyn Hamilton)*

108 Sussex Gardens, **Gordon Cummins** *(Doris Jouannet)*

109 Bryanston Square, **Harry Lewis**

110 Stourcliffe Street, **Derek Lees-Smith**

111 *Norfolk Street,* **François Courvoisier**

112 Park Lane, **Marguerite Diblanc**

113 Cadogan Place, **William Marchant**

114 Lowndes Square, **Ernest Walker**

115 Lowndes Square, **Patrick Mackay** *(Adele Price)*

116 Cheyne Walk, **Patrick Mackay** *(Isabella Griffiths)*

117 Eaton Place, *Sir Henry Wilson*

118 *William Mews,* **Mrs Barney**

119 *Chelsea Fields,* **Edward Jefferies**

120 *Chelsea farm land,* **Weil, Weil, Lazarus & Levy**

121 Gloucester Road, **John George Haigh** *(the McSwans)*

122 Onslow Gardens, **Gunther Podola**

123 Sloane Street, **Roy Fontaine**

124 Beaufort Gardens, **Ley & Smith**

125 Finsborough Road, **Ronald True**

126 Finborough Road, **Cyril Epton**

127 Westbourne Grove, **Horace Rayner**

128 Leinster Square, **Gunther Widra**

129 *Rillington Place,* **John Reginald Christie**

130 Pembridge Court Hotel, **Neville Heath**

131 Chepstow Place, **Grondkowski & Malinowski** *(Reuben Martirosoff)*

132 Clarendon Road, **Dr Norman Rutherford**

133 Ladbroke Grove, *James Pope-Hennessy*

134 Addison Road, *Vera Page*

135 Elsham Road, **Harold Trevor**

136 *Imperial Institute,* **Madha Lal Dingra**

150 *Clifton Gardens,* *Thomas Anderson*

MAP D

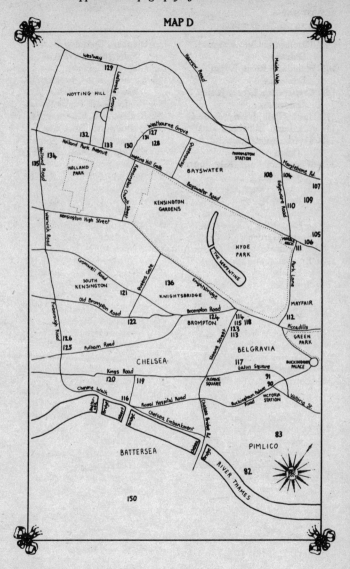

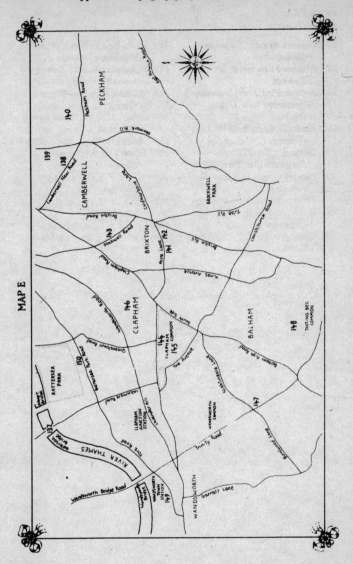

KEY TO MAP F

NORTH LONDON

151 *Greenberry Hill,* Sir Edmund
     Berry Godfrey

152 *Belsize Park walls,* Thomas
     Hocker

153 Avenue Road, Mrs Tierney

154 Park Village East, Adam
     Ogilvie

155 *Pratt Terrace,* Esther
     Hibner

156 *St Paul's Road,* Phyllis
     Dimmock

157 Hawley Crescent, Samuel
     Furnace

158 *Priory Street,* Mrs Pearcey

159 Hilldrop Crescent, Dr
     Crippen

160 Tollington Park, Frederick
     Seddon

161 Seven Sisters Road, Ronald
     Marwood

162 *Bismarck Road,* George
     Joseph Smith

163 Millfield Cottage, Thomas
     Sharpe

164 South Hill Park, Styllou
     Christofi

165 South Hill Park, Ruth Ellis

166 *Black Ditch,* Thomas
     Cooper

167 Danbury Street, Annie
     Walters

168 Islington Green, Fred
     Murphy

169 Noel Road, *Joe Orton*

170 Rock Street, Patrick Mackay
     (Frank Goodman)

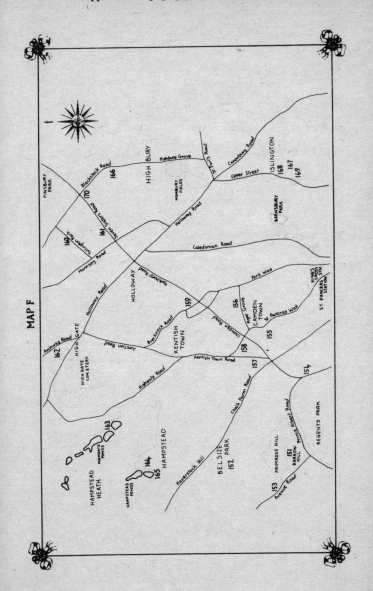

MAP F

FINSBURY PARK

Blackstock Road

HIGH BURY

Highbury Grove

St Paul's Road

Canonbury Road

ISLINGTON

168
167
169

166

170

Upper Street

HIGHBURY FIELDS

Holloway Road

BARNSBURY PARK

Tollington Way

161

160

Hornsey Road

Caledonian Road

Hornsey Road

Holloway Road

HOLLOWAY

Holloway Road

Rothsay Road

York Way

KING'S CROSS STN

159

156

Pooe Grove

St Pancras Way

ST PANCRAS STN.

Archway Road

HIGH GATE

HIGHGATE CEMETERY

Brecknock Road

KENTISH TOWN

Camden Road

CAMDEN TOWN

155

162

Junction Road

Highgate Road

158

Kentish Town Road

157

Chalk Farm Road

154

163

HIGHGATE PONDS

HAMPSTEAD

164

165

HAMPSTEAD PONDS

HAMPSTEAD HEATH

Haverstock Hill

BELSIZE PARK

152

PRIMROSE HILL

151

BARROW HILL

Prince Albert Road

REGENTS PARK

153

Avenue Road

Select Bibliography

MURDER COLLECTIONS AND CRIMINAL BACKGROUND

Altick, Richard D., *Victorian Studies in Scarlet*, Dent, 1970.

Bleakley, Horace, *The Hangmen of England*, Chapman & Hall, 1929.

Butler, Ivan, *Murderers' London*, Robert Hale, 1971.

Gaute, J. H. & Robin Odell, *The Murderers' Who's Who*, Harrap, 1979.

Goodman, Jonathan, *Posts-Mortem: The Correspondence of Murder*, David & Charles, 1971.

Green, Jonathan, *The Directory of Infamy*, Mills & Boon, 1980.

Hartman, Mary S., *Victorian Murderesses*, Robson, 1977.

Honeycombe, Gordon, *The Murders of the Black Museum*, Hutchinson, 1982.

Jackson, Stanley, *The Old Bailey*, WH Allen, 1982.

McConnell, Jean, *The Detectives*, David & Charles, 1976.

Nash, Jay Robert, *Look for the Woman*, Harrap, 1984.

Sellwood, Arthur, *The Victorian Railway Murders*, David & Charles, 1979.

Smyth, Frank, *Cause of Death: The Story of Forensic Science*, Orbis, 1980.

Tomkinson, Martin, *The Pornbrokers*, Virgin, 1982.

Tullett, Tom, *Strictly Murder*, Bodley Head, 1979.

Wilson, Colin, *A Criminal History of Mankind*, Granada, 1984.

– and Pat Pitman, *Encyclopaedia of Murder*, Arthur Barker, 1961.

– and Donald Seaman, *Encyclopaedia of Modern Murder*, Arthur Barker, 1983.

INDIVIDUAL BIOGRAPHIES, CASES & MEMOIRS

Anderson, Sir Robert, *Criminals and Crime*, Nisbet, 1907.

– *The Lighter Side of my Official Life*, Hodder & Stoughton, 1910.

Anon, *The Edgware Road Murder*, Duncombe & Co, 1837.
- *The Trial of Weeping Billy for the Murder of Ann Webb, etc.*, London, 1807.
Bavin, Bill *The Strange death of Freddie Mills*, Howard Baker, 1975.
Bridges, Yeseult, *Poison and Adelaide Bartlett*, Macmillan, 1970.
- *Two Studies in Crime*, Hutchinson, 1959.
Browne, Douglas G. & E.V. Tullett, *Bernard Spilsbury: His Life and Cases*, Harrap, 1952.
Celebrated Trials Series, David & Charles, 1971.
Clark, Tim & John Penycate, *Psychopath*, Routledge & Kegan Paul, 1976.
Cornish, G.W., *Cornish of the 'Yard'*, John Lane, 1935.
Cullen, Tom, *Autumn of Terror*, Bodley Head, 1965.
- *Crippen: The Mild Murderer*, Bodley Head, 1977.
Dew, Walter, *I Caught Crippen*, Blackie, 1938.
Du Rose, John, *Murder Was My Business*, Mayflower, 1973.
Firmin, Stanley, *Crime Man*, Hutchinson, 1950.
Foot, Paul, *Who Killed Hanratty?* Cape, 1971.
Jackson, Robert, *Francis Camps*, Hart-Davis, McGibbon, 1975.
Kennedy, Ludovic, *10 Rillington Place*, Gollancz, 1961.
Knight, Stephen, *The Killing of Justice Godfrey*, Granada, 1984.
La Bern, Arthur, *Haigh: The Mind of a Murderer*, WH Allen, 1973.
Leeson, Ben, *Lost London*, Stanley Paul, 1934.
Linklater, Eric, *The Corpse on Clapham Common*, Macmillan, 1971.
Lucas, Norman, *The Lucan Mystery*, WH Allen, 1975.
- *The Monster Butler*, Arthur Barker, 1979.
MacNaghten, Sir Melville L., *Days of My Years*, Edward Arnold, 1914.
Notable Trials Series, William Hodge, 1921–60.
Odell, Robin, *Jack the Ripper in Fact and Fiction*, Harrap, 1965.
Rumbelow, Donald, *The Complete Jack the Ripper*, WH Allen, 1975.
- *The Houndsditch Murders*, St Martins, 1973.
Samuel, Raphael, *East End Underworld: Chapters in the Life of Arthur Harding*, Routledge & Kegan Paul, 1981.
Simpson, Keith, *Forty Years of Murder*, Harrap, 1978.
Skelhorn, Norman, *Public Prosecutor*, Harrap, 1981.
Tullett, E. V., *No Answer from Foxtrot Eleven*, Michael Joseph, 1967.
- *Portrait of a Bad Man*, Evans, 1956.
Warren, Sir Charles, 'The Policing of the Metropolis', *Murray's Magazine*, IV:23, 1888.
Wensley, F. P., *Detective Days*, Cassell, 1931.

West, Donald J. and Alexander Walk, *Daniel McNaughton: His Trial and Aftermath,* Gaskell, 1977.

Whittington-Egan, Richard, *A Casebook on Jack the Ripper,* Wiley, 1975.

Williams, John, *Suddenly at the Priory,* Heinemann, 1957.

INDIVIDUAL CASES: BACKGROUND ONLY

(I reject the conclusions reached in the following books.)

Bridges, Yseult, *How Charles Bravo Died,* Macmillan, 1970.

Clarke, T.E.B., *Murder at Buckingham Palace,* Robert Hale, 1981.

Critchley, T.A. & P.D. James, *The Maul and the Pear Tree,* Constable, 1971.

Farson, Daniel, *Jack the Ripper,* Michael Joseph, 1972

Knight, Stephen, *Jack the Ripper: The Final Solution,* Harrap, 1976.

McCormick, Donald, *The Identity of Jack the Ripper,* Arrow & J. Long, 1970.

SOURCE MATERIAL

Broadsheets, Ballads & Cuttings (Two folio scrapbook collections), British Library.

Post Office London Directory

The Times 1800–1983

LONDON TOPOGRAPHY AND HISTORY

Bebbington, Gillian, *London Street Names,* Batsford, 1972.

Besant, Sir Walter, *Survey of London.*
  – *London City,* A & C Black, 1910.
  – *North of the Thames,* Black, 1911.
  – *South of the Thames,* Black, 1912.

Booth, Charles *et al, Life and Labour of the People in London: Third Series: Religious Influences, vols 1–6,* Macmillan, 1902.

Lillywhite, Bryant, *London Coffee Houses,* Allen & Unwin, 1963.

Walford, Edward, *Greater London* (4 vols), Cassell, 1893–95
  – and Walter Thornbury, *Old and New London* (6 vols), Cassell, 1879–85.

MAPS

In:

Besant, Sir Walter (above)
Booth, Charles *et al* (above)
London A–Z, Geographers' A–Z Map Company, 1985.
London De Luxe A–Z Street Atlas and Index, Geographers' A–Z Map
    Company, 1984.
The Perambulator: or Book of Reference and Guide to Every Street etc,
    London, 1832.
Post Office London Directory, Kelly, 1840–.
Smith, Sir H. Llewellyn *et al*, *New Survey of London Life and Labour*,
    vol. IV, P.S. King, 1932.

- Index of Murderers and Victims -

Murderers (convicted and alleged) in **bold**

Maps indicated by letter

Index of Places

Murder Sites in **bold**

Obsolete place names and vanished sites in *italic*

—